Old Stories, New Insights

Searching Bible Women's Stories for Today's Applications

by

Judith Warren Hawkins

Old Stories, New Insights-2nd Edition
by Judith Warren Hawkins

Edited by Paulette Goodman and Reggenia Baskin

Printed in the United States of America

ISBN 9781613797501

Unless otherwise indicated, Bible quotations are taken from the King James Version.

www.xulonpress.com

Table of Contents

Now all these things happened unto them for examples:
and they are written for our admonition, upon whom the ends
of the world are come.

1 Corinthians 10:11

INTRODUCTION

*B*ible women have a lot to say, if we would just listen. In their stories and experiences we learn that Solomon was right, *There is no new thing under the sun* (Ecclesiastes 1:9). While the times and settings are different, the issues of womanhood, the burdens of being female, and the choices as defined by gender were as much a part of their lives as they are for women today.

This examination of 13 Bible women is an in-depth study of how they faced and handled being women in Bible days. Strangely enough, we find there is much we can learn from them. Their journeys into sacred writ highlight that women are valued and loved by God. For example, Hagar yells that God is aware of everything done to us; David's wives show how God uses women to further His sovereign will; Hannah's tears and frustration remind us that God cares and acts; and the woman with the issue of blood confirms God's compassion.

Through the writing of this book, I heard these women answering some of my heart's deepest questions. My prayer is that during your devotional time with them over the next 90 days, they do the same for you.

HAGAR

DAY 1

BIBLE TEXT: Genesis 16:1 *Now Sarai Abram's wife bare him no chil-dren: and she had an handmaid, an Egyptian, whose name was Hagar.*

BIBLE REFERENCES: Genesis 12, 16, 21, 25

---

*H*agar, Sarai's handmaid, is our first case study because Hagar's story illustrates fundamental lessons we must learn if we are to make progress on our spiritual journey. We must both intellectually understand and emotionally accept that "God sees us," cares about us, knows where we are, hears our prayers, and will answer them in the best way, at the best time.

From Genesis 12 we deduce that Hagar most likely joined Abram's family when she was given to him by the Egyptian Pharaoh. Abram lied about his relationship with Sarai and when God revealed to Pharaoh the deception, Pharaoh gave Abram many gifts and gladly sent him on his way.

Some scholars think that Hagar was related to Pharaoh, and thus had a comfortable lifestyle. It is difficult to imagine that she would ask or desire to leave her secure palace home to be a handmaid for the wife of a wandering man, who could not be trusted to even tell the truth about his relationship with his wife.

Ten years after arriving in Canaan, the Promised Land, Abram and Sarai's promised son still had not been born. Was it lack of faith, a desire to have two wives, or just a lack of backbone to deny Sarai that caused Abram to cooperate with his wife's suggestion that Hagar become a second wife to bear the long awaited son?

Again, Hagar had no voice in the decision-making of others which completely and totally impacted her life. And so it has been in our lives. Granted, we always have the ability to choose how we will respond to circumstances and events, but many times we cannot alter or change the underlying decisions. We do not want natural disasters to destroy our homes, nor do we desire sickness or death for those we love and cherish, but life happens. And sometimes, life deals us a heavy hand of misery, strife, disappointment, pain, suffering, tears, and the like.

In these dark moments, our focus must shift outside of ourselves to the larger picture and the bigger questions. "What is God up to? What is He doing? How can I help Him accomplish His purposes?" God yells to us, *Before I formed you in the belly, I knew you and before you were born, I ordained your life* (Jeremiah 1:5).

Sometimes we should just sit and ponder how God orchestrates our lives and brings about His purposes. It is mind boggling to think that each of our forebears had to be in our line of ancestry in order that we might be born. Our spouses had to be at just the right place and at the right time for our lives to intersect and the seed of love to be planted in our hearts.

I am a judge today because God negatively impacted the

financial success of my private law practice so that the thought of running a campaign would become a reality. He increased the office rent at one place so that I would move to what became the perfect campaign headquarters. Key people were available to support and campaign for me only in that time frame.

And how do I know this is so? Because as soon as I announced my candidacy, He released the income revenue taps. If they had been released all year, I would not have considered being a judge at that appointed and anointed time.

DAY 2

BIBLE TEXT: Genesis 16:4 *And he went in unto Hagar, and she conceived: and when she saw that she had conceived, her mistress was despised in her eyes.*

BIBLE REFERENCES: Genesis 12, 16, 21, 25

---

*I*t seems only fair that Hagar should get to settle the score with Abram and, especially, Sarai for putting her in a position of power. They should have thought about Hagar's possible reactions before they decided to use her as a surrogate womb. Did they not know that their way of helping God out, while seemingly the right thing to do, was the way of death (Proverbs 14:12)?

Maybe they were blindsided because a new and different Hagar appeared after she became pregnant. But on the other hand, Hagar could have reasonably concluded that because they believed so much in their great and awesome God, He must have meant for things to play out just as they did.

In Hagar's mind, it was her heathen Egyptian gods who had smiled on her. Instead of being doomed to a childless existence as Sarai's handmaid, she was elevated to second wife and mother of Abram's first-born son. Why should she have any regard for Sarai?

But the Bible also speaks to Hagar, *Pride goes before destruction, and an haughty spirit before a fall* (Proverbs 16:18). God dealt with each of them for their respective culpability in the mess they created. Abram, like Adam, chose his wife over God's expressed will. Sarai, like Eve, thought she had a better idea. Initially, Hagar's fate, like the children of Adam and Eve, was nothing more than collateral damage, but the family's discord was too severe to ignore.

Maybe Abram had second thoughts about his participation in Sarai's plan. The child might be a girl or would not be the promised son. So, it could have been easy for Abram to acquiesce to letting Sarai deal with Hagar as she saw fit since it was her idea that created the mess with Hagar. Deal with it? Sarai did so by dealing harshly with Hagar. Did Sarai secretly regret her plan to help God out? Was she hoping and praying that Hagar would just leave and take that unborn child with her, anywhere but there with Abram and Sarai?

We can be so like Sarai (and Abram)! Our best laid plans backfire on us and we learn too late that God does not need our help to fulfill His promises to us. We should also be careful who we intend to put on the gallows. As Haman learned in the book of Esther, the gallows we build for another may be used for our own demise.

At the end of my first term as judge, a prosecuting attorney ran against me. I was not at all enthused about a contested re-election campaign. All election campaigns are hard work, time consuming, and expensive. I felt that some of my opponent's tactics were unprofessional and mean-spirited, but I lived through the process and was re-elected.

Six years later, my previous opponent campaigned for another judicial position. The very same observations I had made and shared

with her about our campaign turned out to be the very same actions
that resulted in her having to withdraw from the new judge's race.

DAY 3

BIBLE TEXT: Genesis 16:7 *And the angel of the Lord found her by a fountain of water in the wilderness, by the fountain in the way to Shur.*

BIBLE REFERENCES: Genesis 12, 16, 21, 25

I am indebted to the women of the House of Comfort and Refuge Ministries in Havana, Florida, for giving me an opportunity to extract lessons from Hagar's story as I prepared for their theme "God AOL (always on line)," modified to "God AOL, with GPS (guidance, protection, and solutions)."

AOL is the Internet provider whose business model implies that one can always access the Internet via its connection services. GPS stands for global positioning satellite, which allows anything that contains a GPS chip to be located in real time. The chip may be put into cars, credit cards, cell phones, and even implanted in pets.

Hagar's solution to her dilemma was to leave; so she ran away, probably to the relief of Sarai and Abram. But in her journey back home to Egypt, God sent an angel to her by a fountain of water in the wilderness on the way to Shur, which was almost in Egypt.

It is baffling why we sometimes limit God's GPS, even though He says, *Before they call, I will answer; and while they are yet speaking, I will hear* (Isaiah 65:24). Hagar's story debunks the notion that God does not know or care about us, believers and non-believers as well.

Hagar may have been of royal lineage, a daughter of Pharaoh. She would not have been a worshipper of Abram and Sarai's God. Yet, notice in Genesis 16 that Hagar's story, interestingly, does not confirm that she prayed at any time during her running away or that she was frightened by the angel when God's GPS located her in the wilderness. Obviously, living in Abram's household had taught her some things about his God.

How does this insight bring hope to those who pattern their lives after Christ? By our example, we should show others an image of a loving, yearning, caring, and seeking God, so when God appears, they may say, like King Nebuchadnezzar exclaimed, *Lo, I see four men loose, walking in the midst of the fire, and they have no hurt; and the form of the fourth is like the Son of God* (Daniel 3:25).

How easy it is for us to devalue or underestimate the worth of a consistently loving and loveable Christ-centered life. Often the Christian has no idea of the eternal value of doing everything to the glory of God (1 Corinthians 10:31). No matter what our profession, we can report for duty in God's workforce. I like to begin each workday by announcing to Him that I am reporting for duty.

My first assignment as a new county court judge was in traffic court and one of my very first sentencing cases involved a defendant with a long list of DUI charges. He should have been charged with a felony DUI, which is not within the jurisdiction of county court. The sentence I imposed was so peculiar and specific for the defendant that the sheriff sent word they could not implement any more such sentences. The sheriff's deputies were responsible for transporting the defendant to counseling sessions and supervising his progress.

Four years later I learned the rest of the story. The peculiar and specific sentence had yielded the family's long awaited, hoped for results. The man had stopped drinking, was steadily employed, had purchased a home, and had become an AA group leader and sponsor. Finally, the defendant and his family experienced an alcohol free home.

DAY 4

BIBLE TEXT: Genesis 16:8 *And he said, Hagar, Sarai's maid, whence camest thou? and whither wilt thou go? And she said, I flee from the face of my mistress Sarai.*

BIBLE REFERENCES: Genesis 12, 16, 21, 25

---

*T*he angel called Hagar by name and position. Since he already knew her name, rank, and location, why was he asking her questions? For whose purpose were the questions necessary? Could it be that Hagar needed to hear herself answer the questions? He asked her two questions; she only answered one—where she was going. How often we are clear about from whence we came, but a little foggy about where we are going.

In our Christian journey, we can become quite literal when it suits our purposes. We can also act as if we have a hearing problem and, sometimes, we will even play the lack of comprehension card. The obvious literal answer to the second question was "Egypt." But, somehow, Hagar knew that was not what the angel was asking and we give her credit for not insulting the angel. This dialogue is similar to Moses' conversation with God when God called Moses at the unconsumed burning bush (Exodus 3). When God asked Moses what was in his hand, Moses replied, "*A rod*" (Exodus 4). But in following God's instruction to throw down the rod, Moses learned that his rod became the Rod of God to set the Israelites free.

Thus, Hagar's answer to "Where will you go?" required her to realize that she was taking Abram's son from the tents of God to the city of gods.

God is very good at sending us situations or people, angels if He must, to ask us where have we come from and where are we going? These are hard questions, and God means them to be so. How else can He get us to stop and consider our ways? Until we answer both questions, we have no idea of what we are exchanging or giving up. From a hot pot we may be jumping directly into the flames.

There is also another benefit in answering God's questions— they prepare our hearts to obey the instructions which are sure to follow.

When I was an early teen, I decided that no one cared about me. I decided that there was no room for me because my older sister, Juanita, was perfect. The long awaited first girl in the family, she was obedient, cooperative, responsible, played the piano, and had everything going for her. I was simply just Judith Ann, marching to the beat of a different drummer. (Now, of course, there was no objective data to confirm my conclusions.) I distinctly remember telling God that I could do whatever I wanted to do because no one cared or expected anything great and wonderful from me. I fully expected to be the family's black sheep.

But God sent my eighth and ninth grade home economics teacher, Mrs. Owens, to ask me, "Where are you coming from and where are you going?" In her patient, attentive way she taught me to sew, but what she really gave me was a sense of self-value and self-determined purpose. I realized that marching to the beat of a different drummer did not require me to leave my parents' safe boundaries in order to live a successful life.

DAY 5

BIBLE TEXT: Genesis 16:9 *And the angel of the Lord said unto her, Return to thy mistress, and submit thyself under her hands.*

BIBLE REFERENCES: Genesis 12, 16, 21, 25

---

*H*agar was neither frightened by nor disobedient to the angel's instructions to return and submit to Sarai. Not only is God always available, but He is also ready with guidance to help us successfully meet whatever challenges we face.

No doubt this is probably "a do or die" lesson, hard for most of us to learn. Why must we do it His way? Why can't God just place His stamp of approval on our proffered solutions to our problems? Why can't He just allow us to continue with our running away plan as we head back to where we left? Besides, who asked Him to intervene in the first place? We are quite content with our well-thought-out action plans! So many "whys," all answered by a simple and clear word from Him, "Do this . . . " Why? Because He promised in Psalm 32:8, *I will instruct thee and teach thee in the way which thou shalt go: I will guide thee with mine eye.*

In Genesis 16:9, the angel gave Hagar very specific instructions: *Return to thy mistress, and submit thyself under her hands.* Yuck! Not only does God make His instructions simple and clear, He often makes them something we do not want to hear or do! Yuck! Yuck! Yuck!

But when we choose to obey, God gives His divine power which enables us to obey, even if we have an ugly attitude! It is the work of the Holy Spirit to empower us to obey, even to the death of our most cherished and longed-for desires. Like the disciples, whom Jesus told to "tarry" in Jerusalem until the Holy Spirit filled them with power from on high (Luke 24:49), we also have a choice to make. Either we obey and tarry, or we disobey and do not tarry.

I have discovered that only when referring to God can I use the absolutes of "always, everything, every time, everywhere, any time, any place, etc." His Word is sure and can be relied upon. His instructions are based upon His knowing the end from the beginning; thus, while the instructions make absolutely no sense to us, in our submission to His will and His way, we find safety and peace in spite of what our eyes can see and our hearts can feel.

A good friend shared with me the "enmity prayer" based upon Genesis 3:15, which she prayed over her children, especially as they began to date and look for spouses. Praying this prayer is wise and seeks wisdom because it invites God to give guidance to our children (and others we love) by placing a heaven-born discomfort between them and anyone who comes into their space who is not good for them.

As my son Jason dated, I expressed no opinions to him about the young ladies. But I asked them just a simple question, "Did Jason tell you I pray the enmity prayer?" It saved me from offering unwanted and unsolicited advice. The more discomfort I had with the young lady, the more often I would "bother" God with the enmity prayer. I knew that Dionne, my wonderful daughter-in-law, was the right one when I had to "remember" to pray the enmity prayer.

DAY 6

BIBLE TEXT: Genesis 16:10, 11 *And the angel of the Lord said unto her, I will multiply thy seed exceedingly, that it shall not be numbered for multitude. And the angel of the Lord said unto her, Behold, thou art with child and shalt bear a son.*

BIBLE REFERENCES: Genesis 12, 16, 21, 25

---

*G*od's instructions can be trusted because He backs them up with His personal guarantee of power, majesty, and glory. We are safe in following His instructions because with His instructions comes protection from everyone and everything who would seek to interfere with our successful compliance with "Thus saith the Lord." Only God can say that He *is a strong tower,* [where] *the righteous runneth into it and is safe* (Proverb 18:10), or that He is *our refuge and strength, a very present help in trouble* (Psalm 46:1).

Hagar needed encouragement to return and submit to "mean" Sarai. God met Hagar at her point of need by giving her a glimpse into her immediate future. Her unborn child was a boy, who would be blessed because he was Abram's son.

However, Hagar's experience does not bind God to give us revelations about the outcomes, should we choose to follow His instructions. For Hagar He went the extra step, but many of us have to learn that "faith grows by exercise!" Only as we begin the journey does the next step become apparent, and some level of understanding of why the journey is necessary may be revealed—or maybe not! Just ask Job.

When we grasp for anything to understand why we must return and submit to some seemingly overwhelming challenge in our lives, and there is no revelation of what the outcome will be, we must trust what we do know about God. At those times, we must pray back to God His promises, which are so freely placed throughout the Bible. Times of peace and comfort are the perfect times to visualize what we would do in a storm. What promise texts would we claim? What songs would be our battle cry? That's why there are practice fire drills and the like.

Getting married or having a child is a great example of walking by faith. Our best laid plans, our brightest hopes, all of our energy and preparation can prove inadequate to deal with the experiences which, on our worst days, we could never have imagined. It would be wonderful if God, in such times, would give us Hagar's experience and just send an angel who clearly tells us what to do and gives us confirmation that we can rely upon the instructions.

I began writing this book while on Christmas vacation in the Dominican Republic as my husband, Jim, and I celebrated our 35th wedding anniversary. We celebrated our 25th wedding anniversary on the 26th because we were equally surprised that we actually made it through 25 years together. When asked the secret to reaching 35 years, I offhandedly replied, "We just stayed each day and didn't leave—that day!"

Jim and I started our lives together believing in each other's commitment to love and cherish the other and "leave and cleave" (Genesis 2:24). When storms come, all we can do is visualize and practice our emergency response: PUSH (Pray Until Something Happens)!

DAY 7

BIBLE TEXT: Genesis 16:11 *Call his name Ishmael; because the Lord hath heard thy affliction.*

BIBLE REFERENCES: Genesis 12, 16, 21, 25

God named Hagar's child; it is the first time He named a child. The baby would be called Ishmael, "God shall hear."

By naming Ishmael, God committed Himself to Hagar as her own personal God. No longer would she rely upon Abram's mercy or his provisions. From that day forward, Hagar had tangible evidence that God was merciful and would graciously intervene to meet her needs.

Likewise, we also are well known to God. God saw Hagar's afflictions and heard her prayer, whether she prayed aloud or in her heart as Samuel's mother, Hannah, did when she asked God for a son (1 Samuel 1).

At some point we must "tell God all about it." Whether we are burdened by cares, overworked, overstressed, overlooked, abused, misused, underpaid, undervalued, devalued, despised, unforgiven, unmentioned, unconsidered, whatever (there's that absolute again), we can tell God all about it—and He hears and will do something about it, in the best time and in the best way.

In the meantime, while we are waiting and hoping that God will rend the heavens and come down (Isaiah 64:1), we must follow

David's example when he *was greatly distressed; for the people spake of stoning him, because the soul of all the people was grieved, every man for his sons and for his daughters: but David encouraged himself in the Lord his God* (1 Samuel 30:6).

During the middle years of my marriage, it appeared that a divorce was just a judge's signature away. The Lord spoke to me and specifically told me to "Keep your mouth closed." That was a challenge, because I wanted so badly to let Jim have it with both barrels of my loaded and cocked emotional gun. But God also told me how to obey. He said, "Walk." I remember becoming quite physically fit during that year. I would walk early in the morning, in the early evening, and, sometimes, during the midnight hour.

I soon noticed that there was a pattern to my conversations with God during those walks. The first third of the way, I just ranted and raved about how unfair and wrong this whole family break-up was. The second third of the trek, the Holy Spirit would show me things from another perspective; He was changing my paradigm. And the final third, was a time of exhaling, accepting, and submitting to doing it God's way—which, first and foremost, was to keep my mouth closed!

No, it wasn't easy. Yes, it was hard and painful. But I have a moment in time that forever makes Hagar's experience my own.

DAY 8

BIBLE TEXT: Genesis 16:12 *And he will be a wild man; his hand will be against every man, and every man's hand against him; and he shall dwell in the presence of all his brethren.*

BIBLE REFERENCES: Genesis 12, 16, 21, 25

---

*K*nowing for sure what the future holds is not necessarily a good thing. The future can be rather dark and bleak, hopeless, and seemingly without an end to the trials of life. No wonder God commanded Joshua to be strong, be courageous, and not to be afraid in Joshua 1. God promised to be with him wherever he went. That's an absolute promise, "wherever." Because of God's absolutes we can submit to David's instructions, *Wait on the Lord: be of good courage, and he shall strengthen thine heart: wait, I say, on the Lord* (Psalms 27:14).

Based upon Israel's up and down future, Joshua would have agreed with Hagar that it was a good thing the guidance and protection aspects of God's GPS were manifested before the rest of the story was revealed. Ishmael's future, as revealed to Hagar, probably was not exactly as she had anticipated. Mary, Jesus' mother, did not understand the hows and whys of His life, and if she had, it would have made His death by crucifixion all the harder to bear.

How often we lie to ourselves when we demand God to show us the future. The cares and worries of today are crushing us and we want to know the specifics of the future! Really now! What we are really saying is, "Lord, confirm for us that it will end up all good." With our limited spiritual eyesight, we usually only want to see good in our future. Why? Because we look at our lives with microscopes and God uses His omnipotent telescope that takes Him to the end of time.

Just shy of her 48th birthday, my sister, Jennifer, died from a rare form of cancer. We were a family of ten: three brothers, five sisters, and two parents, and we each had our very own request of God about her condition. Jennifer was academically challenged, so her employment options had been quite limited.

My parents' concern was that she would outlive them and their ability to shore up her financial circumstances. Juan, the eldest brother, wanted her to be with her sisters when death came. James, III, the pastor, wanted confidence that her future was hid in Christ. Juanita, the eldest and most tightly connected sister, needed to be present when Jennifer closed her eyes the last time. Joseph, the prayer warrior, wanted her death to be easy.

Jennifer lived in Tallahassee, Florida, under my care. It was very important to me that her death not be a long, slow process. Jennifer herself wanted to be independent until the end. Joyce, who had the successes Jennifer desired, wanted Jennifer to die knowing that Joyce valued and loved her for who she was. And Justina, the nurse, wanted Jennifer to die without pain.

The family gave God such a long list of competing requests

about the future, yet God answered each and every one of them. We saw in her passing God's tender compassion, enabling each of us to "be strong and of good courage."

A dark future was brightened by God's presence.

BIBLE TEXT: Genesis 16:13 *And she called the name of the Lord that spake unto her, Thou God seest me: for she said, Have I also here looked after him that seeth me?*

BIBLE REFERENCES: Genesis 12, 16, 21, 25

---

*A*s we accept and cope with learning that in His loving mercy God limits our foreknowledge of the future, we are free to give new names to our experiences. Naming something or someone is a personal and satisfying experience, whether it is a car, a dear one, a not-so-dear one, a pet, or a child.

God named Ishmael to confirm that God hears our cries. Now it was Hagar's turn to give God a new name, and she called Him "El Roi," which means "The God Who Sees Me."

When the angel met Hagar, he addressed her as Sarai's handmaid, which indicated that the angel knew exactly who she was. But God's angel knew much more. He knew that Hagar was proud and haughty and that the harsh treatment she received from Sarai was in direct response to Hagar's uppity attitude and spirit. He knew that in choosing to return to her old life in Egypt, she was prematurely leaving the place God wanted her to be, not learning the lessons she needed to learn, and not doing what He wanted her to do—to be Sarai's handmaid. From then on, Hagar knew that God saw her, on the outside as well as on the inside. He had plans for her life.

When our son Jason was a little boy, he loved for me to tell him over and over again that five years before he was born, he existed in our hearts. We knew that we would have a son and his name would be Jason. Somehow, I think that's also the reason why we did not have any other children; Jim and I could not agree on any names!

Names are important, and whether we are aware of it or not, it is a proven fact that we internalize what others think of us, based upon what they call us. It is a mistake to think that "sticks and stones may break my bones, but words will never hurt me!" It is interesting to note the difference between a child's given name, which the parents may have spent months choosing, and the nickname, which arises either from some event in the child's life or from a characteristic of the child.

Far too often, children (and adults) are emotionally starved for someone to call them by a term of endearment or to give them a name of promise and expectation. And have we ever noticed that addressing another by an endearing name when we are furious with him or her seems to soften the anger? How angry can one really be when calling the other person, "Honey," "Precious," or "Dear"?

DAY 10

BIBLE TEXT: Genesis 21:9 *And Sarah saw the son of Hagar the Egyptian, which she had born unto Abraham, mocking.*

BIBLE REFERENCES: Genesis 12, 16, 21, 25

---

*F*ast forward about 14 years—Isaac, the son of promise, had been born, Abraham and Sarah had new names, and it is pretty clear from the way Ishmael is not named that things had been rough for Hagar and her son.

Hear the contempt in Sarah's voice as she said that Ishmael was *the son of Hagar the Egyptian, which she had born unto Abraham.* Sarah could have said she "saw Abraham's first-born son, Ishmael, making fun of Isaac." From Sarah's words we would think that Sarah had nothing to do with all the drama created by her insistence that Abraham father a son with Hagar.

As the angel instructed, Hagar had returned and submitted to Sarai. Over the years, Hagar fondly watched as Abram bonded with Ishmael, but not too closely because Sarai would constantly remind Abram that Ishmael was not the promised child. What a second-class-citizen complex Ishmael and Hagar must have experienced. They were at the table, but not wanted. It makes perfect sense that Ishmael would have negative feelings toward Isaac.

This family curse of jealousy would be played out again in the story of Joseph and his brothers (Genesis 37). Even the disciples struggled for first position in Jesus' coming kingdom (John 13).

The continuing discord in the Middle East stems from Ishmael and Isaac, the two sons of Abraham.

Familial generational curses are real, just as familial generational blessings are real. It requires an enormous amount of focused work and commitment to break curses and strengthen blessings. The argument over which influence is stronger, genes or environment, must acknowledge that our DNA "is what it is." The goal of environment is to "re-program" our natural responses so we can improve our chances of making better choices and controlling the natural propensities transferred through our DNA. The best defense in stopping generational curses and promoting generational blessings is changing one person at a time.

Of all my court assignments, I prefer the criminal divisions because defendants must heed the court's instructions or suffer predictable consequences. And precisely because of that fact I am able to "encourage" radical changes in defendants' participation in their future through education. Underage traffic court defendants are assigned significant community hours, which may be "worked off" by improving their high school grades. Often, these students return to my courtroom with straight "As" and with a new "can do" attitude.

Pregnant women without GEDs are also given the option of obtaining their GEDs in lieu of performing all the community service hours. Pursuing a GED is regularly added to defendants' probation terms. They are impressed with themselves when they report back to court with GEDs in hand.

One defendant obtained his GED under the court's encouragement and was inspired to continue his education at the local community college. Only eternity will tell the ripple effects of his changed life.

DAY 11

BIBLE TEXT: Genesis 21:10 *Wherefore she said unto Abraham, Cast out this bondwoman and her son: for the son of this bond-woman shall not be heir with my son, even with Isaac.*

BIBLE REFERENCES: Genesis 12, 16, 21, 25

---

*H*agar must have asked God why He had not let her return to Egypt some 14 years earlier. Hagar had not asked to be included in Abraham's family. The facts were clear—Sarah demanded that this bondwoman and her son be cast out! What happened to Hagar's status as the second wife?

Hagar safely concluded that Sarah never liked her after she became pregnant with Ishmael, so it was easy for Sarah to demand that they be put away from Isaac. Once again, Hagar was sucked into the consequences of Sarah and Abraham's decisions. And, it clearly appeared that they did not care about or give one thought to the ramifications for Hagar and Ishmael.

It was Sarah and Abraham's deceit that had turned Hagar's world upside down. They heaped insult upon insult when they decided that Hagar would be Abraham's second wife. Hagar had not been able to regain control over her destiny. Either Sarah, or an angel, or Abraham told her what she had to do.

I imagine that Hagar was stunned. Surely it had crossed her mind that Sarah would soon die and then Hagar and Ishmael would take their rightful places, she as the new wife and Ishmael as the first-born son. Now, Sarah wanted them cast out! Abraham was her only hope. What would he decide?

When my siblings agreed to move our parents to Tallahassee, where I live, we expected them to live out their golden senior years in their own home with minimum needs for caregivers. We had no idea that as their mental faculties declined, competing issues for their care would necessitate unwanted solutions. Mother suffered from small, deeply-embedded strokes. They affected her enough that she required constant supervision.

Father, her husband for more than 50 years at the time, felt that he was capable of adequately providing for her care. He made it difficult for us to keep hired help to care for mother. Of course, he thought he didn't need any help.

When we found both of them on the floor one morning because she had fallen and he couldn't get her up, it was clear that they could no longer live together without 24/7 care. Because he wouldn't allow round-the-clock care in the house, we had no other option than to put mother in a nursing home. Our father's care for himself deteriorated rapidly; he needed to live in an assisted living facility.

During my early adult years, my grandfather lived with my parents. Later, my mother lived in Oklahoma with my grand-aunt. I wonder if my parents ever expected that they would be placed in group living facilities as their children experienced circumstances they neither could change nor control. Hagar's dilemma . . .

DAY 12

BIBLE TEXT: Genesis 21:12 *God said unto Abraham, Let it not be grievous in thy sight because of the lad, and because of thy bond-woman; in all that Sarah hath said unto thee, hearken unto her voice; for in Isaac shall thy seed be called.*

BIBLE REFERENCES: Genesis 12, 16, 21, 25

---

*A*s Hagar waited for Abraham's response to Sarah's demand, her only hope was that finally he would stand up to Sarah and protect Ishmael. Abraham had not done right by Hagar from their first encounter in Egypt. Was Abraham just "hen-pecked"? Did Sarah hold all of the decision-making authority in the home?

Ishmael had been Abraham's only son for the last 14 years and they had bonded. Abraham's love for his first-born son was strong enough that this time he would not yield to Sarah's demand. Finally, Abraham showed backbone and hope flooded Hagar's heart. Then God finally spoke to Abraham about the Hagar saga, and, once again, Hagar has no say about what is being done to her. Would her entire life be on the receiving end of other people's cavalier decisions which would have monumental impact upon her?

Hagar probably had some choice words for God because He had done nothing when Sarai suggested that Hagar become Abram's second wife, nor had God spoken when Sarai dealt with Hagar. How could God, who had spoken directly to Hagar requiring her to return and submit to "mean" Sarai, not even bother to give Hagar at least a heads-up on Ishmael's future after Isaac's birth? Then Hagar could have better prepared Ishmael.

Hagar bobbed and weaved among whom she was most angry with—Ishmael, Sarah, Abraham, or God?

Many married couples have a defining argument or moment when each knows whether the relationship will last until death, or until the divorce papers can be filed, however long the time between the decision to leave and the actual divorce. As a Florida board certified family law attorney, my practice allowed me to talk to many spouses about when the decision to leave was actually settled in their minds. Clients told me that the decision was made on the honeymoon night, or as they walked down the aisle, or during the marriage ceremony, but the divorce was 25, even 45 years later.

Over the years I decided that there was a correlation between the insignificant items the parties fought over and the intensity of each spouse's processing the winding down of their marriage. The more emotional investment a spouse had in the relationship, the more traumatic the break-up. I concluded that the cheaper the cost of the item, the more the item was a symbol of some deep emotional experience or quality of the relationship. Or the more sentimental the item, the harder it was to let go of the memory attached to the item.

For example, a wife's letting go of the coffee pot meant accepting that there would be no more early morning talks over coffee because the husband would no longer prepare the coffee as a part of their waking up ritual. The coffee pot represented her joy and pleasure, now turned to pain and loss. Or consider a wife's agreeing to let the husband have the heirloom quilt from his side of the family, which required her letting go of her status and relationship with his family.

DAY 13

BIBLE TEXT: Genesis 21:14 *And Abraham rose up early in the morning, and took bread, and a bottle of water, and gave it unto Hagar, putting it on her shoulder, and the child, and sent her away: and she departed, and wandered in the wilderness of Beersheba.*

BIBLE REFERENCES: Genesis 12, 16, 21, 25

"Thanks, God!" Hagar cried as she and Ishmael left the security of their home, moving into their unknown future. Abraham did not even bother to give them parting gifts. Hagar herself had been a parting gift from Pharaoh to Abram; surely they were entitled to more than just some bread and water! Based upon their status, Abraham owed each of them things of value. She was a bondwoman, handmaid, wife, and mother of Abraham's first-born. Ishmael was his first-born son. Under any category, they deserved more than bread and water sufficient only to get them to the next well.

What insults God's chosen patriarch had heaped upon Hagar and that same God was responsible for Hagar's now helpless state. "I don't ever want anything to do with You, and anything that reminds me of the years spent, no, wasted under Abraham's tents, will be stench in my nose," Hagar sobbed as she and Ishmael, a teenager, left behind the only home Ishmael had ever known.

Sometimes, God's calls are so painful because they require a total exchange of the known for the unknown. Unrecognized and unappreciated by Sarah, Hagar, like Abraham, was being called to a place she knew not where, but there God Himself would greet her and meet her needs. But she did not know that—yet.

How do we leave our comfort zones? "Some are called, some are sent and others got up and went," it has been said. Maybe we get the choice to accept the mission as Abraham did or maybe the mission is "dumped" upon us as with Hagar. But the call is loud and clear—there is something somewhere else God wants us to experience.

I vaguely remember that as a toddler I would leave home. Without adult assistance or supervision, I crossed the street to Mrs. Patterson's house. At five I went to Mrs. Kirby's house and at 13 to Ms. Thomasina's home. I attended four colleges during my four years of college, including Newbold College in England. Maybe that's why it was easy for me to find the perfect gift to give God when I turned 50.

The gift had to be personal and require minimum consent or permission from others. I combined my love of "going" with service. My first outing was to help build a school in Costa Rica, but I realized that the trip was not about my building schools; it was for me to meet Pastor Robert Folkenberg, who had just started a program where laity would use outlined PowerPoint sermons and preach around the world. His dream was that they would be inspired to preach in their own countries and churches. That explains how I have preached in Kenya, Dominican Republic, Taiwan, Romania, Mongolia, Papua (Indonesia), and Havana, Florida.

God calls each of us. What is your answer?

DAY 14

BIBLE TEXT: Genesis 21:15, 16 *And the water was spent in the bottle, and she cast the child under one of the shrubs. And she went, and sat her down over against him a good way off, as it were a bow shot: for she said, Let me not see the death of the child. And she sat over against him, and lift up her voice, and wept.*

BIBLE REFERENCES: Genesis 12, 16, 21, 25

---

*H*agar had nothing to say to God. Things had gone from bad to worse, and they appeared to be worsening. It was His fault—all His fault. It was evident that He agreed with Sarah; Ishmael was a nuisance and needed to die. To ensure his death, Hagar concluded, God had a backup plan. Abraham had given Hagar and Ishmael enough water and bread to make it to the next well. Was it God's plan for them to die in the dry hot wilderness? What an amazing similarity between Hagar's experience and what the Israelites would encounter on their journey from Egypt to Canaan!

Hagar's new critical test depended upon her understanding of Abraham's God, but based upon everything she had experienced, Abraham's God was symbolic of pain, loss, and disappointment. Frustrated because she was helpless to do anything about her situation, she had a "meltdown," a "pity-party," a good cry. How short our memories are of God's interventions in our lives. Hagar had "been there, and done that." She was in the wilderness—again! She was concerned about her child—again! She was without human help or support—again! She was headed back to Egypt—again! The only incident missing was an appearance by an angel—again!

When I was a middle school aged child, I grasped the concept of tithe paying. When I put my first dime of tithe into the offering plate, I reminded God that He said, *Bring ye all the tithes into the storehouse, that there may be meat in mine house, and prove me now herewith, saith the Lord of hosts, if I will not open you the windows of heaven, and pour you out a blessing, that there shall not be room enough to receive it* (Malachi 3:10).

As soon as the Sabbath was over, I ran to the corner store and used my left over pennies in the bubble gum machine. In those days there was a speckled ball worth five cents. I got one. I was impressed. Then I got another. My dime of tithe had been returned to me! I was forever convinced and convicted that tithe paying was "a good thing."

But as we grow up, financial responsibilities crowd our plates such that child-like faith in God keeping His promises is considered childish. Besides, many Christian budgeting programs do not teach Biblical principles of tithes and offerings. And some preachers say, "Tithing is not important as long as you pay your dues."

Yet, when our income is finished before the month ends and that is the pattern month after month, year after year, then something is amiss. Our bread and water run out in our financial desert.

Like Hagar, we should leave our entangled financial messes about an arrow's bow shot away, as we cry out to God in utter frustration.

DAY 15

BIBLE TEXT: Genesis 21:17 *And God heard the voice of the lad; and the angel of God called to Hagar out of heaven, and said unto her, What aileth thee, Hagar?*

BIBLE REFERENCES: Genesis 12, 16, 21, 25

What was Ishmael saying that got God's attention over Hagar's cries? Why was God more willing to respond to his voice rather than Hagar's? How could Ishmael's situation demand more and get immediate attention? As if God was rubbing salt into Hagar's wounds, why did He have to make it so clear that it was all about Ishmael? "Hagar," God said, "because of Ishmael's voice I am checking on you." God could have just kept that editorial comment to Himself!

How often we have been blessed because God heard and answered another's prayer on our behalf. While living in Sodom, Lot, Abram's nephew, was taken captive (Genesis 14). God blessed Abram's rescue of Lot, the other captives, and their goods. In response to Abram's concerns about a reprisal attack, the Bible records the first "Fear not" as God assured Abram that He was his shield and He would exceedingly and greatly reward Abram for serving Him (Genesis 15:1).

So for whatever the reason, an angel communicated with Hagar, again! Before, the angel's questions were designed to make Hagar articulate her situation and her issues (Genesis 16), but this time

Hagar had already articulated her situation and issues. She was willing to die from thirst and hunger, but to see her only son die was just too much. Thus, the cause of her bitter tears and loud crying.

When our son was eight years old, he was diagnosed with Crohn's disease, a mysterious chronic aliment identified by inflammation of parts of the small or large intestines (but may include any part of the digestive system). Jason's symptoms were in his lower colon, which often caused high fevers, weight loss, severe constipation, and rectal bleeding. All medical examinations were painful—as were his attempts to use the bathroom. We had difficulty finding a local doctor who would treat him, and any medical attention in Tallahassee was directed by the physicians from Shands, the University of Florida Hospital in Gainesville, Florida.

During one of Jason's exams conducted in Tallahassee, I vividly remember standing outside the examination room as his screams could be heard halls away. Like Hagar, I just cried out to God for some relief for my child. I would gladly take his disease. A local gastroenterologist whom I knew just happened to pass by at that time and I asked him if there was anything he could to do help us. He said that he would take Jason as a patient.

That's when we learned about the limitations of managed health care insurance. Even though he was a local specialist, the managed health care insurer refused to authorize him to treat Jason. We changed health insurance providers, which opened doors for Jason to receive more appropriate and helpful care.

DAY 16

BIBLE TEXT: Genesis 21:17 . . . *fear not; for God hath heard the voice of the lad where he* is.

BIBLE REFERENCES: Genesis 12, 16, 21, 25

"*Fear not*," the angel said to Hagar. This is the second time in the Bible comfort is issued with these words. How interesting that "Fear not" was first spoken by God Himself to Abram when God confirmed His promise to bless Abram's seed (Genesis 15), and next to Hagar when God confirmed His promise to bless Abram's first-born seed, Ishmael.

When spoken to Abram, "Fear not" allayed his fears about the consequences of Lot's experiences with which Abram had nothing at all to do. When the angel spoke "Fear not" to Hagar, it allayed her fears about Abram and Sarai's experiences which were thrust upon her. God spoke "Fear not" to Isaac when he, like Abram, lied about his relationship with his wife, and God assured Isaac that he would be blessed in spite of the mess he created (Genesis 26).

The fourth "Fear not" was spoken by the midwife to Rachel as she struggled to deliver Benjamin. This time God used a woman to confirm that His promise to Abram would come true as the midwife said to Rachel, *Fear not, thou shall have this son also* (Genesis 35:17). The fifth "Fear not" Joseph's steward spoke to Joseph's nine brothers on their second journey to Egypt to purchase grain (Genesis

50). God was twice removed in delivering the message of "Fear not," but as before, it was based upon God's original promise to Abram.

It really does not matter how God chooses to confirm in us, "Fear not." Whether it is spoken directly to us by God Himself, or via His angel, or via another, or via the authority of another, "Fear not" means just that—exhale and trust God to keep His promises.

Participating in international mission work is my passion, but it sometimes requires long flights which are often marked by air disturbances causing frightening moments in the plane. Almost instantaneously when the plane begins to bounce around in the air, I hear God speaking to me, "Fear not, you are on my errand and this plane will not go down."

Another concept we glean from the first five "Fear nots" is that whatever our situation, God still says to us "Fear not." It does not matter if someone else created the mess, we created the mess, or the mess was thrust upon us; in the midst of it, God says, "Exhale and fear not."

DAY 17

BIBLE TEXT: Genesis 21:18 *Arise, lift up the lad, and hold him in thine hand; for I will make him a great nation.*

BIBLE REFERENCES: Genesis 12, 16, 21, 25

*A*fter the angel of God spoke "Fear not" to Hagar, he gave specific instructions—again. Hagar—again—had to decide whether to obey, without any more assurance than the angel's word that all would be well. She was to retrace her arrow's bow distance back to the shrub where Ishmael was crying and dying, lift the emaciated teenager into her arms, and repeat to him what the angel said without adding the words, "Although you are about dead from thirst and hunger . . ."

Why does "Fear not" come with instructions when all of our senses tell us it is a good time to bolt and run, like Jonah, in the opposite direction? Mirrored in Hagar's experiences are Abraham's experiences, albeit, the difficulty may appear lessened, but from Hagar's point of view, her experiences were as trying and testing as Abraham's refining fires. Maybe God is clearly affirming that He places value upon women's involvement in the fulfillment of His eternal promises and will.

As God promised to bless Abram's seed, so God promised Hagar that her seed would be blessed. As Abram journeyed to a place he knew not, so Hagar's journey ended where she knew not. As Abram relied upon God to protect him in Canaan, so Hagar relied upon God to protect her under Sarai's oppressive hand. As Abraham had Mount Moriah, so Hagar had the wilderness. Both sons were offered up to death. Both lads were miraculously saved.

It is only in our explicit obedience that "Fear not" means "Fear not." The assurance is a light to our path and a boundary for our feet only as we stay in the highlighted and marked way.

My friend, Nina, says that being fearful means we have no faith. I say that fear is summed up in the acronym:

False

Evaluation

About

Reality, which is what God sees, not our point of view.

In obedience to God's leading and word, the divine power knocks fear out of us, as if (when) our breath has been knocked out of us. We are momentarily stunned and dazed; we are not really with it nor are we totally out of it. For a moment, our lives pass before us and we either exhale confidently that God's "got it" or we hyperventilate with panic, trying to get a hold on it.

The opportunities to obey are as many as the moments of each waking day. Do we first have private worship or begin the morning's tasks? Do we submit our "to do list" to God or demand that He accomplish everything on it according to our prioritizing? Will we go back to the place where we looked on hopelessly and helplessly as something we valued was dying, and lift it up and hold it in our hands, just as the angel instructed?

DAY 18

BIBLE TEXT: Genesis 21:19 *And God opened her eyes, and she saw a well of water; and she went, and filled the bottle with water, and gave the lad drink.*

BIBLE REFERENCES: Genesis 12, 16, 21, 25

Water! Hagar saw a well of water. Literally, water to drink for their survival, but water also symbolized nourishment to strengthen her belief in God's promise that Ishmael would be a great nation. Only from the place where Hagar lifted up the lad and held him in her hands could she see the well of water. Only on Mount Moriah, at the place where his arm was raised to slay Isaac, would Abraham see the ram in the thicket (Genesis 22).

The Bible is one long story of people being in the "place" where God's will is manifested. But each character had to choose whether to be in the "place." Only from that "place" could they see more clearly God's intentions and will. Isaiah saw "the Lord sitting upon a throne" from the place of King Uzziah's death (Isaiah 6:1). Habakkuk's place allowed him to see Babylon's utter destruction of Israel, yet he wrote, *Although the fig tree shall not blossom, neither shall fruit be in the vines; the labor of the olive shall fail, and the fields shall yield no meat; the flock shall be cut off from the fold, and there shall be no herd in the stalls: Yet I will rejoice in the Lord, I will joy in the God of my salvation* (Habakkuk 3:17, 18).

Likewise, our being out of place causes us to miss seeing what God wants us to see. Consider Adam and Eve, the Antediluvians, and the Jewish leaders during the time of Christ.

Nothing occurs in our lives without God's knowledge and permission. My first international evangelistic campaign was conducted in Homa Bay, Kenya, East Africa. When I left, I never expected to return; yet, less than nine months later, I was back, by way of South Africa.

One of the "place" experiences occurred on my March 2003 flight from Nairobi to Johannesburg when my seatmate asked me if I had been to Kenya before. My journal notes report that I had seconds to decide whether I should just answer with a "yes" or share that I was returning from visiting the place where I had preached the year before. I chose the latter and he shared that he was looking for "that something" he had noticed in other Christians. In response to my seatmate's questions about passion, his priest had pointed him to Stephen Covey's *Seven Habits of Highly Effective People*, a book which changed my paradigm.

As we began our discussion, I pointed him to Covey's pyramid and analogized that putting Christ at the base or the top determines whether a Christian has that something he had observed. When Christ is at the top, it is as if He is a decoration; nice, but not necessary. But when the foundation of the pyramid is Christ, everything else fits into its proper place.

DAY 19

BIBLE TEXT: Genesis 21:20, 21 *And God was with the lad; and he grew, and dwelt in the wilderness, and became an archer. And he dwelt in the wilderness of Paran.*

BIBLE REFERENCES: Genesis 12, 16, 21, 25

---

*R*ather than continuing their journey into Egypt, Hagar and Ishmael settled in the wilderness of Paran, located in the southern part of Canaan. Why?

Maybe it was because Hagar's experiences had resulted in her not being welcomed in Abraham's house, and after being gone from Egypt twenty-four years or so, she did not think that she would be welcomed or comfortable there. Maybe her family was no longer in power and there really was not a "home" to return to. Maybe Ishmael was a "wild child" and he needed a free environment. Maybe she had had it with communal living. Or maybe, she just preferred the "living by your wits" wilderness life style.

While it seems harsh to describe Hagar as a "misfit," she probably was a sojourner, looking for a place where she belonged.

That has a familiar sound, *By faith Abraham, when he was called to go out into a place which he should after receive for an inheritance, obeyed; and he went out, not knowing whither he went* (Hebrews 11:8). In Hagar and Ishmael, we continue to see direct analogies to Abraham's experiences.

I remember as a child thinking to myself that I was so unlike my siblings, I had to have been adopted! I just did not want to follow the pattern my four older siblings had established. I wanted nothing to do with my parents' practical advice about education and career choices or their "how to get along with people" skills.

Each Sunday morning my father conducted family council. My parents with their eight children sat around the formal dining room table and discussed family business, which included upcoming events and our wants and needs. Most times those needs were requests for money for some school related item or clothing. We were required to submit written proposals in support of our requests, which included cost estimates as well as alternative plans should our requests be denied during family council. My father was teaching us to prioritize limited resources.

I must have been about 14 when my proposal was for a pair of shoes. I really wanted those shoes and was sure that my request would be granted. It was not! My disappointment turned into anger as I vowed that I would never again give the family council authority to validate my wants and needs. I would earn my own money to buy my own shoes and anything else I desired.

During that time my mother sold Avon products. That very Sunday afternoon I took her materials, went into the neighborhood, and knocked on every door pushing the products. Of course, there were record sales that reporting period. I sold more than enough to buy the pair of shoes!

In hindsight, feeling that I was a "misfit" fueled my energy to persevere along the route I wanted to travel.

DAY 20

BIBLE TEXT: Genesis 21:21 . . . [Hagar], *his mother took him a wife out of the land of Egypt.*

BIBLE REFERENCES: Genesis 12, 16, 21, 25

*H*agar and Ishmael lived in the desert where Ishmael's hunting skills provided for their temporal needs.

Hagar's last deed was to find a wife for Ishmael among her people, as did Abraham in sending his trusted servant, Eliezer, to Abraham's home to find a wife for Isaac (Genesis 24). What criteria did Hagar consider for Ishmael's wife? Apparently, the same as Abraham; Isaac's wife must be of Abraham's kindred and Isaac was not to return to Haran.

The Bible does not disclose anything further about Hagar or her death, unlike the deaths of Sarah, Rebekah, and Rachel. Nor does the Bible provide anything more about Ishmael's wife, but Ishmael had "twelve princes" (Genesis 25:16), while Abraham's grandson, Jacob, had twelve sons (Genesis 35:22). Only heaven's records are complete because like so many who have lived and died, history just gives footnotes about their lives.

Ishmael was 14 years older than Isaac and was banned from Abraham's tents. Ishmael was 74 when Isaac's twins were born, 89 when Abraham died, and Ishmael was 137 when he died.

Parents usually aim to do their best for their children, taking seriously their responsibilities to nurture and to lead by example. Of course, what they mean may be said louder in their attitudes and by their actions than in their words.

But our children are not us! Although parents may attempt to "cookie cut" them, children are distinctly unique and different from their parents. Children's gene pools include everyone in their genetic history. They also adapt to environments, customs, and cultures. We exclaim with David, [We] *will praise thee; for* [our children are] *fearfully and wonderfully made* (Psalms 139:14).

When our Jason returned home for his first holiday break from college, we sat at the kitchen table playing Rook, a card game. Jason shuffled the cards with such ease and skill that I asked him when and where he had mastered that skill, fully expecting him to say that he had learned it at college, indicative that he was not wisely using and managing his time.

Instead, he replied that while a 10th grader at the local high school, he gambled away his lunch money playing cards. Stunned, I asked, "How did you eat?" "Oh," he replied, "I just got more lunch money from you and Dad."

I had no idea of his foray into the world of card shark gambling. "What happened?" I asked. Just as casually, he replied, "I got tired of losing more and more money, so I stopped."

Parents ought *to always pray and not to faint* (Luke 18:1).

DAY 21

BIBLE TEXT: Genesis 25:12 *Now these are the generations of Ishmael, Abraham's son, whom Hagar the Egyptian, Sarah's handmaid, bare unto Abraham.*

BIBLE REFERENCES: Genesis 12, 16, 21, 25

*I*t is appropriate that we end the study of Hagar, whose name means "flight," as the Bible ends her story. Her flights had taken her into personal encounters with the God of Abraham.

In Genesis 25, we learn that after Sarah's death, Abraham married Keturah, who gave him six sons. Abraham also had sons by concubines, and to these sons he gave gifts and sent them away. At Abraham's death, the Bible only acknowledges Ishmael and Isaac as Abraham's sons.

In Genesis 12, we assume that Hagar entered Abram and Sarai's lives as a handmaid, a gift from Pharaoh. In Genesis 16, Hagar became Abram's wife; yet, even Hagar did not recognize that status, because she referred to Sarai as her "mistress" when she met the angel at the well of Shur. The angel confirmed her assessment of her status when he instructed her to return to Sarai, her mistress.

In Genesis 21, both Abraham and Sarah refer to Hagar as a "bondwoman," a term of contempt indicating slave status, due no respect, affection, or consideration. The slaves and servants could be and often were treated as members of the family; Abraham initially thought to treat Eliezer, the steward of Abraham's house, as his heir (Genesis 15).

Hagar received no respect, recognition, consideration, or appreciation from Sarah or Abraham. She was a "throw-away" person within their small closed community. We can definitely conclude that from the day Sarai decided to interfere with God's plans to give Abram the promised son, Hagar was used and abused.

No doubt Hagar did not ingratiate herself to Sarai. Hagar had an attitude in her responses to the circumstances in which she found herself. It is reasonable to conclude that life was not fair to Hagar. But God made lemonade from the bitter lemons in her life.

Genesis 25, the last reference to Hagar, confirms that God kept His promise made to her at the well at Shur; through Ishmael, God exceedingly multiplied her seed so that it could not be counted.

Handmaid, wife, bondwoman, whatever the title, Hagar shares with us her experiences with "El Roi," the God who saw her.

And, God also sees *me*. Nothing hides *me* from God's eyes; no situation, no circumstances, no problem, nothing.

HANNAH

DAY 22

BIBLE TEXT: 1 Samuel 1:2 . . . [Elkanah] *had two wives; the name of the one was Hannah, and the name of the other Peninnah: and Peninnah had children, but Hannah had no children.*

BIBLE REFERENCES: 1 Samuel 1, 2

---

*O*ur second case study is Hannah, whose life shared many of Sarah's experiences noted in the study of Hagar. Hannah was Elkanah's first wife, whom he deeply loved and cared for, as Sarah was loved by Abraham. Both women were barren and each husband had children by second wives, who taunted them, making Hannah and Sarah's lives miserable. But God miraculously intervened, giving each a promised son, which brought great rejoicing and celebration.

Elkanah, Hannah's husband, was a Levite of the family of Kohath, who lived with the tribe of Ephraim (1 Samuel 1:1). Their children would be the descendants of Korah, who challenged Aaron's appointment as priest for the Israelites during the Exodus from Egypt (Numbers 16). In response to Moses' prayer, God's prompt response to Korah's rebellion demonstrated that God can and will do a "new thing" to confirm those who agree with and to convict those who challenge His sovereign will.

Hannah's name means "graciousness" and "favor," but her image of herself was shaped and defined by her having no children. She saw no favor in her childless life, and graciousness was a heavy burden to carry in her situation. Regardless of what "virtuous woman" traits (Proverbs 31) Hannah possessed, none could counterbalance her state of childlessness.

Hannah was in a double-bind. She saw herself as unblessed and Peninnah, the other wife, delighted in taunting and reminding Hannah of her barrenness. Her life was miserable.

Before becoming a judge, I represented parents accused by the State of Florida of abusing, abandoning, or neglecting their children. I represented an 18 year-old mother who threw her infant son into the air, allowing him to fall on his head. The mother was the product of various states' foster care systems. Under Florida laws, termination of parental rights requires children to be taken into state custody and no further services are provided to the parents.

Preparing our defense, the mother and I chose the doctor who completed the mother's psychological assessment. That evaluation would make or break the mother's case. As the doctor testified about the emotional state of the mother, it was clear that she needed intensive and extended mental health counseling. Her needs were so great, the doctor testified, that it would be at least two years before minimum supervised contact between the infant and the mother could begin.

The Court terminated parental rights and as I pondered the implications of that decision, I instinctively knew that the mother would continue to have children. Because there was no reunification plan with her first child, I knew that she would bear her future children without any help for her underlying psychological issues.

There are so many unwanted children or children whose parents are unable to care for them. Each woman who has children should desire them like Hannah.

DAY 23

BIBLE TEXT: 1 Samuel 1:5 . . . *the Lord had shut up* [Hannah's] *womb.*

BIBLE REFERENCES: 1 Samuel 1, 2

*E*ach year, Elkanah and his family probably made three 12-mile journeys from Ramah to Shiloh to worship at the temple where Eli, the priest, served with his two sons, Hophni and Phinehas. Elkanah provided adequate portions of meat to Peninnah and her children, but he gave double portions to Hannah, treating her as if she had a child.

A divine revelation about a situation often enables, encourages, and helps us to bear the test. Thus, the Bible's interlinear comments give us an advantage that many Bible characters did not have as they went through their experiences. Consider Job, who did not know that God and Satan had conversed about him (Job 1 and 2). But to the contrary, Amos, the prophet, wrote that God is also just as likely to explain and warn us about His plans (Amos 3:7).

Like Sarah, Elizabeth, and the Shunammite woman, God had shut up Hannah's womb (Genesis 16, Luke 1, and II Kings 4). Each of these women had no idea why or even that God had intentionally chosen to deny them their culture's most highly valued attribute of womanhood, i.e., motherhood. In some cultures today, motherhood is just as valued and defining of women as it was in Bible times;

while in other societies, motherhood is rejected as the standard by which women's contributions are measured. Some reasons for this change include more women participating in the marketplace and women's rights to self-determination.

It is absolutely true that God does not make mistakes and each person's life is well known to Him. As David exclaimed in Psalm 8, God cares so much about humans that He is mindful of us, visits us, and crowns us with glory and honor.

When my judicial assignment includes the child support enforcement docket, I want God to give me insight into the future of many of the children whose parents, usually fathers, refuse to provide financial support. The children can greatly suffer.

Sometimes I ask the mother how many of her children were fathered by the respondent. Then I inquire how many children the respondent had before her children. My next question is telling. Was the respondent financially responsible for those other children? That answer is almost a 100% predictor as to the respondent's commitment to provide for this mother's children.

Of course, there are the mothers who had no reason to suspect that upon the termination of the relationship between the parents, the father would also chose to financially abandon his children.

Even if the culture and society place a high value on motherhood and demand that fathers be financially responsible, there is still much wisdom in a woman having only as many children as she can adequately support.

DAY 24

BIBLE TEXT: 1 Samuel 1:6, 7 *And her adversary also provoked her sore, for to make her fret, because the Lord had shut up her womb. And as he did so year by year, when she went up to the house of the Lord, so she provoked her; therefore she wept, and did not eat.*

BIBLE REFERENCES: 1 Samuel 1, 2

---

*M*aybe this is how Hannah's name got its meaning. Hannah remained gracious in spite of Peninnah's relentless bragging and "one-upmanship" because she had children and Hannah had none. Mothers name their daughters Hannah, but I've never heard of a Peninnah.

From the text, we can safely imply that during the trips to Shiloh Peninnah's proud spirit especially soared to a higher level; her words and attitude toward Hannah intensified in frequency and maliciousness. It is hard to endure ridicule and harassment for things that we do, but to relentlessly be tortured about things over which we have no control, *only* God's grace can enable us to endure graciously.

The Bible does not go beyond the reference to Peninnah's actions, but we can safely imply that Peninnah's children observed their mother's words and actions toward Hannah. Peninnah was teaching her children to disrespect and devalue Hannah because of her childlessness. This also must have added to Hannah's pain and sorrow, for when she sought to discipline Peninnah's children, their replies would be something like, "What do you know? You don't have any children!"

And there is also another message that Peninnah was sending to her daughters; if they, like Hannah, did not have any children, Peninnah's daughters would be disrespected and devalued by Peninnah! Children derive their core self-esteem and evaluation of themselves from their primary caregivers.

Both as a family law attorney and as a judge presiding over dissolution of marriage actions, I routinely discuss with divorcing parents the importance of watching what they say about the other parent, particularly in the presence of their children. When a parent says unkind words about the other parent, *even if true*, the children listening can and do translate those sentiments to themselves. They are one-half of that other "no good" parent.

DAY 25

BIBLE TEXT: 1 Samuel 1:7 *So* [Peninnah] *provoked* [Hannah]; *therefore she wept, and did not eat.*

BIBLE REFERENCES: 1 Samuel 1, 2

---

*H*annah responded to Peninnah's constant badgering with tears and loss of appetite. She was distraught and oppressed. Clinically depressed would be an appropriate diagnosis for Hannah's response to Peninnah's barbed words and mean spirited attacks. But Hannah was also weighed down because Peninnah's words were true; she was indeed childless.

"Sticks and stones may break my bones, but words will never hurt me" is a handy rhyme mothers teach their children in attempts to deflect the pain that belies the rhyme. But words do hurt and it is a toss-up whether the true words or false words hurt more.

What do we do and where do we go for comfort and refuge when all about our world is crumbling and sinking sand, as an old spiritual song asks? The refrain answers joyfully, "I go to the Rock, the Rock of my salvation." Whether the source of our distress comes from within or without, the only way to remain upbeat and positive is to follow David's example, *From the end of the earth will I cry unto Thee, when my heart is overwhelmed: lead me to the rock that is higher than I* (Psalm 61:2).

My eighth grade home economics teacher, Mrs. Owens, taught

71

us that people bite their nails and have eating binges on unhealthy foods when they are nervous, worried, and stressed. I did both. But one day in her class I vowed to myself that never again would someone be able to look at my nails or my waistline and deduce that I was unhappy or fretful. I would never again be without a nail clipper, and *bags* of apples became my stress relief food of choice.

Many years later, I saw a movie about a couple's break-up and watched as the wife "let herself go," spiraling down into deep depression and grief. One day in the grocery store she had an "aha" moment and determined to pull herself out of the dumps.

Then, my marriage hit the rocks. Only if people knew my coping strategies could they have rightly concluded the depth of my struggles. I walked one to three miles, two or three times a day, and ate lots of fruits, particularly *bags* of apples. Compliments about my trim body and healthy complexion confirmed that my cover up was working.

Now, when I have a craving for apples, extra exercise, or have an obsession with my nail clipper, I stop, look, and listen. I want to know what's bothering me!

DAY 26

BIBLE TEXT: 1 Samuel 1:8 *Then said Elkanah her husband to her, Hannah, why weepest thou? and why eatest thou not? and why is thy heart grieved? am not I better to thee than ten sons?*

BIBLE REFERENCES: 1 Samuel 1, 2

---

*E*ven if Elkanah's words rubbed salt into Hannah's wounds, they came from his sincere desire to be attentive and supportive, traits which are still highly valued in human relationships. The questions are also trick questions! The last question puts the other questions into context; Hannah really could not answer her husband. How could she agree that Elkanah was better than ten sons? If she did, then she should not be sorrowful about her barren condition. If she said no, Elkanah was not better than ten sons, then she would have to admit that her love for her husband was motivated by her desire to be a mother. Elkanah's comforting words placed her between a rock and a hard place!

Not necessarily intentionally, but sometimes comforters cause us to experience more pain. The Bible reports Job's comforters as examples of "bad" comforters. Solomon, the wisest man who ever lived, encourages us that comfort may come from friends who are closer than family (Proverb 18:24). Yet when our spirits are heavy and it seems no one can comfort us, Jesus anticipated those "nights of weeping" and left us the best Comforter, His Holy Spirit

(Psalm 30:5; John 14).

I read about a student pastor who sought to comfort his teacher after his wife's death from cancer. After the funeral, the student pastor wrote a note to his teacher, in which he "shared some theological thoughts that [he] thought would be helpful to him in his loss. [The teacher's] response stunned [the student pastor]. 'Don't you ever do that to anyone again!' he said. 'None of that theology is worth a piece of manure right now. You don't know what it means to lose your wife, and your words only make it worse.'"[i]

As I mulled over those words, my mind went back several years ago to a conversation I had with a friend whose fiancé died in a freak car accident one rainy weekday morning as he drove to work. To her questions about why, I replied that pain and sorrow are the results of Satan's rebellion in heaven and that God grieves with us as we suffer through these rough experiences. Until God *wipes away all tears from* [our] *eyes,* [because] *there is no more death, neither sorrow, nor crying, neither pain: for the former things are passed away* (Revelation 21:4), our days will be filled with grief and grieving.

I wonder if she thought to herself, "Your words only make it worse . . ."

DAY 27

BIBLE TEXT: 1 Samuel 1:9, 10 *So Hannah rose up after they had eaten in Shiloh, and after they had drunk. Now Eli the priest sat upon a seat by a post of the temple of the Lord. And she was in bitterness of soul, and prayed unto the Lord, and wept sore.*

BIBLE REFERENCES: 1 Samuel 1, 2

*A*fter the feast, which gave Peninnah another opportunity to harass Hannah about her childless state, and Elkanah's sincere offer of confused affirmation, Hannah went to the temple. That Eli, the priest, was seated by a post of the temple was of no concern to Hannah, for she was in deep distress. Her mind was so burdened and heavy that she was simply unaware of another's presence. The intensity with which Hannah approached God reveals much about the intensity of her pain and longing. Hannah had a Garden of Gethsemane experience (Mark 14).

At first glance, the word "bitterness" seems inappropriate in this context, because "bitterness" is a negative emotion, characterized by anger, resentment, and resentfulness, emotions hard to picture Hannah possessing. Was she resentful? Was she angry? Was she filled with resentfulness?

R. T. Kendall writes in Chapter One of *Total Forgiveness*[ii] that "Bitterness is an inward condition. It is an excessive desire for vengeance that comes from deep resentment. It heads the list of the things that grieve the Spirit of God." Hannah's "bitterness of soul" accurately described the heavy, dark, oppressive clouds enveloping her. She wanted relief; she needed help. She did not want to live another day without hope.

It was in the temple that she sought help and hope. She took her emotions, whatever they were, in prayer mixed with tears straight to God. Hagar's story does not present her as seeking God; God came to Hagar, probably because Hagar had no background reference for Jehovah. But Hannah had learned from birth about the merciful God who miraculously brought Israel out of Egyptian bondage. Our lives provide us too many opportunities to share Hannah's experience; thus, with bitterness of soul we pray and uncontrollably weep before God about our health, our spouses, our children, our workplaces, our parents, our finances, our delayed dreams, and busted hopes.

Sometimes during church services, our "bitterness of soul" swells up within and bursts out in cries mixed with praise and prayer. We may be embarrassed by our own or others' sudden release of sound, but in that moment, like Hannah, we cease to be aware of anyone or anything around us. We share Jeremiah's experience—the pain or praise within our spirit is like the loud popping sound of fire shut up in our bones (Jeremiah 20:9).

Whether in private or in public, in order to share Hannah's lack of awareness of others or Jeremiah's response, we must experience "bitterness of spirit," weeping sorely, with or without audible sounds, crying to God . . .

DAY 28

BIBLE TEXT: 1 Samuel 1:9, 10 *And she vowed a vow, and said, O Lord of hosts, if thou wilt indeed look on the affliction of thine handmaid, and remember me, and not forget thine handmaid, but wilt give unto thine handmaid a man child, then I will give him unto the Lord all the days of his life, and there shall no razor come upon his head.*

BIBLE REFERENCES: 1 Samuel 1, 2

---

*H*annah initiated negotiations with God. She gave Him her best offer. If God would give her a son, she would dedicate her son back to God, confirming her promise by not allowing his hair to be cut, also an indication that her son would be a Nazarite, like Samson and John the Baptist (Judges 13; Luke 1).

Those who took the Nazarite vow did so voluntarily to confirm their consecration or the setting of themselves aside for God's service. Their vows could be temporary or for life. Only Samson's story lists the other components of the vow: abstaining from all products of the grape, including the wine and fruit; allowing hair on the head to grow uncut; and avoiding any contact with dead bodies, including close relatives.

However, three Nazarites mentioned in the Bible were dedicated by their mothers prior to their births. Samson rejected his parents' imposition of the vow upon his life. John the Baptist accepted his parents' vow placed upon his life. Would Hannah's son accept the vow?

In making her best offer to God, Hannah must have known from Samson's story that parents' compliance with God's will does not ensure that the unborn child will likewise submit to God's divine purpose. Yet, the fact that she would make the offer showed the depth of her commitment and desire to have God grant her request. Only time would tell whether she would keep the vow if God accepted her offer to dedicate her yet-to-be-conceived son back to God.

There is no doubt we initiate negotiations with God today.

DAY 29

BIBLE TEXT: 1 Samuel 1:13 *Now Hannah, she spake in her heart; only her lips moved, but her voice was not heard: therefore Eli thought she had been drunken.*

BIBLE REFERENCES: 1 Samuel 1, 2

*E*li rushed to judgment based upon what his five senses perceived. He observed Hannah's moving mouth, but he heard no sound. Apparently, he did not allow his sense of smell to verify his observations, or come close enough to touch Hannah before he spoke his conclusion—Hannah was drunk. While stunned by the priest's absolute lack of pastoral counseling skills, Hannah promptly corrected his misconstruing of her physical and emotional states, explaining that she was not under the influence of alcohol, but rather *a woman of sorrowful spirit, pouring her soul before the Lord, out of the abundance of her complaint and grief* (verses 14-16).

Complaint and compliant—what a difference the order of the letters "a" and "i" make. There is an old saying, "If it quacks like a duck, waddles like a duck, has a beak like a duck, then it is a duck!" How quickly we make conclusions based on first impressions. We misjudge another's actions based solely upon our physical senses.

Eli saved the day when his spiritual senses awakened. In confidence he spoke reassuring words to Hannah, *Go in peace: and the God of Israel grant thee thy petition that thou asked of Him* (verse

17). Hannah "received" Eli's blessing; she *went her way, and did eat, and her countenance was not more sad* (verse 18). She arose early the next morning, worshipped, and returned home to Ramah, where *the Lord remembered her* (verse 19). Upon the birth of her son, she named him Samuel because she asked the Lord for him (verse 20).

Samuel was "conceived" in the temple, when Hannah "received" Eli's words. Hannah's faith anchored onto Eli's prophecy, and in that very moment her empty womb was filled. At that moment, she held her son in her arms and smelled his fresh baby smell. She was no different from the centurion who told Jesus to just speak the words of healing for his servant in Matthew 8.

Reality occurs twice: first in the mind, then in the physical realm.

My son loved for me to tell him how his father and I agreed that one day we would have a son, and we would call him Jason. We were married five years before Jason was born, but when he arrived, it was as if he had always been physically present.

Faith is making up our minds to "see" what our eyes cannot see; faith is giving form and shape to the ideas in our minds. That's why we must be so careful about what we visualize in our minds' eye. But when we ask God for something and He says yes, let's just "receive" it.

DAY 30

BIBLE TEXT: 1 Samuel 1:28 *Therefore also I have lent him to the Lord; as long as he liveth he shall be lent to the Lord.*

BIBLE REFERENCES: 1 Samuel 1, 2

---

*A*s Samuel was "conceived" when Eli blessed Hannah, Hannah "gave back" Samuel before his birth. She "saw" Samuel as "coming through her" on his way to fulfill God's purpose.

The baby was probably just a few months old when Elkanah went back to Shiloh for the yearly offering, but Hannah did not return to Shiloh until Samuel was weaned and ready to begin his training under Eli, the priest. When Hannah took young Samuel to Shiloh, she also took an offering. Over the three to five years it took for Hannah to wean Samuel, Eli probably had forgotten about his encounter with Hannah, so she reminded him that she was the woman he had thought was drunk (1 Samuel 1:21-27).

This was the "rest of the story." Hannah's vow made during her time of great and deep need was remembered and honored. God had accepted Hannah's offer and performed His part of their agreement. Now Hannah completed her obligation under the contract. While Samuel was a child, she returned him to the Lord.

Hannah did not give herself an opportunity to "renege on" or change her mind about her promise. Nor did she delay obedience based upon whatever excuse she thought reasonable to justify her non-compliance with her contract with God. Hannah made her son a living sacrifice, holy, and acceptable unto God (Romans 12:1). Her faithfulness to the vow she voluntarily made to God resulted in rich blessings upon her, the aged priest Eli, Samuel, and the people of Israel.

When Hannah left Samuel with Eli, he blessed Hannah again, telling her that God would give her more children because she had given Samuel to God. The *King James Version* says that "for the loan which is lent to the Lord," God would give them "seed." Imagine, loaning something or someone to God. My father has a saying, "You can never give God too much; if you do, He will repay with interest." Hannah's story ends with the note that God visited Hannah and she had three more sons and two daughters (1 Samuel 2: 20, 21).

We do not always or often remember when and where fundamental lessons are taught or learned. However, at some point in time, Ecclesiastes 5:4 and 5 seeped deeply into my conscious thoughts. Solomon wrote, *When thou vowest a vow unto God, defer not to pay it; for he hath no pleasure in fools: pay that which thou hast vowed. Better is it that thou shouldest not vow, than that thou shouldest vow and not pay.* The point was repeated when Jesus talked in Matthew 21 about the father asking his two sons to work in the vineyard. The first said no, but repented and went to work; the second said yes, but did not do it.

marriage? · Our word should be our bond. Rather than ignoring our promises, we should strive to honor them or be honest enough to say we made a mistake and ask for forgiveness. What changes would occur in our lives this day if we remembered our vows and diligently, intentionally sought to honor them? We would actually pray for the people whom we told we would pray for them. We would make payments against all outstanding loans from family and friends and we would try to make our marriages work.

What blessings are we missing because we have failed to honor a vow we voluntarily made with God during a period of intense negotiations?

DAY 31

BIBLE TEXT: 1 Samuel 2:21 *And the Lord visited Hannah, so that she conceived, and bare three sons and two daughters. And the child Samuel grew before the Lord.*

BIBLE REFERENCES: 1 Samuel 1, 2

And Hannah prayed, and said,

My heart rejoiceth in the LORD,

mine horn is exalted in the LORD:

my mouth is enlarged over mine enemies;

because I rejoice in thy salvation.

There is none holy as the LORD:

for there is none beside thee:

neither is there any rock like our God.

Talk no more so exceeding proudly;

let not arrogancy come out of your mouth:

for the LORD is a God of knowledge,

and by him actions are weighed.

The bows of the mighty men are broken,

and they that stumbled are girded with strength.

They that were full have hired out themselves for bread;

and they that were hungry ceased:

so that the barren hath born seven;

and she that hath many children is waxed feeble.

The LORD killeth, and maketh alive:

he bringeth down to the grave, and bringeth up.

The LORD maketh poor, and maketh rich:

he bringeth low, and lifteth up.

He raiseth up the poor out of the dust,

and lifteth up the beggar

from the dunghill, to set them among

princes, and to make them inherit the

throne of glory:

for the pillars of the earth are the LORD'S,

and he hath set the world upon them.

He will keep the feet of his saints,

and the wicked shall be silent in darkness;

for by strength shall no man prevail.

The adversaries of the LORD shall be broken to pieces;

out of heaven shall he thunder upon them:

the LORD shall judge the ends of the earth; and

he shall give strength unto his king,

and exalt the horn of his anointed.

1 Samuel 2: 1-10

JOCHEBED

DAY 32

BIBLE TEXT: Numbers 26:59 *And the name of Amram's wife was Jochebed, the daughter of Levi, whom her mother bare to Levi in Egypt: and she bare unto Amram Aaron and Moses, and Miriam their sister.*

BIBLE REFERENCES: Exodus 2, 6; Numbers 26

We learn the name of Jochebed, Moses' mother, in Exodus 6 and Numbers 26, as a postscript to the listing of her husband Amram's genealogy. For such an important woman in the Bible, her name and background are provided as an aside, a filler, an afterthought. Sometimes, it seems that the Bible is just too bottomline! On the other hand, the succinctness requires study and comparison of scriptures, since understanding of one text is received through analysis of other texts (Isaiah 28:13). We must be thankful for good concordances and that at least the wives' names were provided, because generally ancient genealogical lists included a woman's name only in exceptional cases.

Jacob's sons are listed by generations, and we are told that *Amram took him Jochebed his father's sister to wife; and she bare him Aaron and Moses* (Exodus 6:20). Amram, son of Kohath, grandson of Levi, great-grandson of Jacob, married his father's sister, his aunt. Prior to the Exodus, there was marriage among family members, including brothers and sisters: *Cain knew his wife* (Genesis 4:17), and Sari was Abram's half-sister (Genesis 12:13; 20:12). God specifically forbade the custom in Leviticus 18:9.

Moses, Jochebed's son, prepared to lead the people of Israel out of Egypt, fulfilling God's promise to Abraham that the fourth generation of those who went to Egypt would return to the Promised Land (Genesis 15:16). There could be no generations without women, named or unnamed.

The Bible's succinct manner of recording history leaves it to us to imagine the "rest of the story" regarding named and unnamed personalities. It forces us to re-assess our evaluation of the characters' worth and contributions based upon the length of their records. By begging the question, the Bible takes for granted the truth of how importance and worth are defined.

My friend, Theresa Hall, tells the story of seeing a little boy on the street and calling him "Sugar" as she spoke to him. His eyes brightened as he asked, "Are you calling me 'Sugar'?" Theresa sweetly replied, "Yes." From his brightened countenance Theresa concluded that he might never have heard anyone refer to him in such a kind and loving manner. For Theresa, the impact of that chance encounter on his life remains only in heaven's records. Yet, it inspired me to make a point to speak lovingly and kindly to children, whenever and wherever our paths should cross.

Others knowing our names for our contributions is nice. But if not, that's okay too.

DAY 33

BIBLE TEXT: Exodus 2:2 *And* [Jochebed] *conceived, and bare a son: and when she saw him that he was a goodly child, she hid him three months*.

BIBLE REFERENCES: Exodus 2, 6; Numbers 26

---

*F*rom the time he was born, Jochebed knew that there was something different about Moses.

Jacob's favorite son, Joseph, was dead when Moses was born. The new Pharaoh, who did not know Joseph, decreed that all the male Hebrew babies were to be killed by one of the two Hebrew midwives. The new Pharaoh perceived that the Israelites were multiplying so quickly that they would eventually take over Egypt. The midwives ignored Pharaoh's directive, so he decreed that all the baby boys should be cast into the Nile River (Exodus 1).

Apparently, some baby boys were dying, but Jochebed determined to save her son and hid him in her home for three months. The tension in the home must have been great as she instructed Miriam and Aaron not to expose the family's secret about little baby Moses. His cries were quickly soothed to avoid arousing the neighbors, any of whom might report Jochebed to Pharaoh.

But she knew that soon her precious little baby would be too big to continue hiding in the house. What was she going to do? How would and could she protect the life of her "goodly child"?

It was as if Jochebed claimed the promise in James 1:5 that when we lack wisdom, we can ask God for it. He will generously and freely give us wisdom. Jochebed needed an original, divinely inspired solution to her problem.

Reality is really a two-step process: when we make up our minds, it is then done; we only wait to "see" it in the physical realm. Years ago when I was in charge of the youth program at church, my overwhelming motivation was for the youth to have new experiences, including camping, banquets, and traveling to youth conventions. Fund raising, of course, was an important component of the leadership. It became obvious that the youth would cooperate and participate in numerous car washes and bake sales because they believed that they would obtain the goal, i.e., doing the activity. Fund raising was not work; it was fun because it confirmed that the idea of the new experience would become reality.

Counselors often advise people to be sure that they seek careers which involve doing what they genuinely like to do. Then work is not work because it is satisfying and rewarding. Making up our minds first allows us to interpret events, people, and circumstances in the light that our ideas are becoming reality.

DAY 34

BIBLE TEXT: Exodus 2:3 *And when she could not longer hide him, she took for him an ark of bulrushes, and daubed it with slime and with pitch, and put the child therein; and she laid it in the flags by the river's brink.*

BIBLE REFERENCES: Exodus 2, 6; Numbers 26

---

*F*inally, Jochebed complied with Pharaoh's order; she cast Moses into the river. However, Pharaoh's command did not say *how* the baby was to be "cast" in the water! Now that was a brilliant solution to her problem—she obeyed Pharaoh!

Before casting Moses into the Nile, she placed him in a watertight basket formed from papyrus and coated with bitumen and tar. She then hid it among the tall reeds which bordered the Nile River. Using what was at hand, Jochebed found the very source of her problem as the solution to her problem. Later, Moses would find that his rod, which was both in and at hand, would be God's solution to many of his challenges in leading the people from Egypt.

Far too often, it is only in retrospective analysis that we comprehend that the solutions to our challenges were in the challenges themselves. Then God's infinite wisdom, which is counter-intuitive, seems so apparent and simple.

With a prayerful heart, Jochebed had obeyed God's instructions for hiding her little one. She could only wait to see how God would reward her obedience.

Frequently, intense discussions arise when one party accuses the other of "splitting hairs," or in utter frustration asserts that the other party knew what was intended. One can hear these arguments when spouses argue and in conversations between parent and child. However, "splitting hairs" is the stock and trade of legal positions. Attorneys argue that what is written or said is subject to multiple interpretations; many a case has been won because the attorney was able to present a plausible alternative interpretation of the law, the contract, or the conversation.

DAY 35

BIBLE TEXTS: Exodus 2:4, 7 *And his sister stood afar off, to wit what would be done to him. . . . Then said his sister to Pharaoh's daughter, Shall I go and call to thee a nurse of the Hebrew women, that she may nurse the child for thee?*

BIBLE REFERENCES: Exodus 2, 6; Numbers 26

*B*etween verses 4 and 7, Jochebed's heart was totally committed to her head. She had obeyed and now could only trust and believe that "El Roi," Hagar's God, would see her in her time of great distress and need. How would God save her baby boy?

Exodus 2:5 and 6 tells how Pharaoh's daughter came to bathe in the river and saw Moses' basket amongst the river weeds. She sent her maid to fetch it and when she opened up the little basket, Moses cried. She instantly knew that she had found a Hebrew baby boy whose mother could not kill her son. Pharaoh's daughter had compassion upon the "goodly" child (Exodus 2:2).

God's hand in the plan was revealed through Miriam, Moses' older sister, who was stationed to keep watch over the little ark. Jochebed had instructed her how to respond to any discovery of the baby. If any Egyptian found the basket, she was to ask if the Egyptian wanted a nursemaid for the child. Quickly, and without fear, Miriam appeared before the princess of Egypt offering to find someone to nurse and care for the crying baby boy.

Does your heart leap within you as you read this? God always has a plan and no matter how foolish it may look to us, He only bids us to obey and trust Him.

When my marriage was in great turmoil, God specifically instructed me to say very little, to literally "close my mouth." It seemed that the "sharing" of my thoughts and emotions greatly interfered with His plans of reconciliation. He assigned me the task of working on puzzles whenever I needed to vent. My *first* puzzle was of a garden scene and was fairly difficult. I finished the puzzle and found that one piece was missing. I searched diligently about the table for the one brown piece. I carefully felt over the completed puzzle, and even wrote a letter to the company hoping to find a replacement for the one missing piece. But the missing piece was not to be found. My alternative plan was to use shoe polish to paint over the missing area.

I saw the missing piece as an omen of the future of our marriage. Even if we survived the storm, our relationship would forever bear the scar of the trauma. We would never be as we were before experiencing the drama of our hearts rending apart. I settled into accepting the reality of that thought and moved forward to frame the puzzle.

After the puzzle glue dried, it was safe to move the puzzle. As I slid the puzzle into the picture frame, the missing piece was uncovered! My heart leapt for joy! The found missing piece was symbolic to me that not only would the marriage survive, but it would be stronger and tighter than before. It was God's sign to me that everything would be all right.

I had determined to keep my mouth closed and God determined to stop a great loss.

DAY 36

BIBLE TEXTS: Exodus 2:8, 9 *And Pharaoh's daughter said to her, Go. And the maid went and called the child's mother. And Pharaoh's daughter said unto her, Take this child away, and nurse it for me, and I will give thee thy wages. And the woman took the child, and nursed it.*

BIBLE REFERENCES: Exodus 2, 6; Numbers 26

The party in Jochebed's home that day was so loud that everyone had to come and determine the reason for the celebration! "El Roi's" plan was so extraordinary and complete—not only was Moses' life spared by Pharaoh's daughter, but Jochebed got paid to rear own her son! It couldn't get any better than that!

Remember, one of the Bible's first "Fear nots" was spoken to Hagar as she and Ishmael faced certain death in the wilderness (Genesis 21:7). From Jochebed's point of view, that text would read something like: And God heard baby Moses crying in a basket, hiding from certain death; and out of heaven, the angel of God called to his anxious mother, and said unto her, "What's the matter, Jochebed? Fear not, for God hath heard the baby's cry from where you hid him amongst the river grass."

In trusting obedience we clearly can hear God say to us, "Fear not." The question is, will we trustingly obey?

While God is omnipresent, He prefers to find us where He

requests us to place ourselves.

My 2007 mission trip took me to Tamika, Papua (Indonesia). The safest place to stay was in the Sheraton Hotel, but it was also more than I wanted to pay for my housing during the two-week evangelistic campaign. Also, my assigned church was about a thirty minute ride from the hotel to an area very close to the Freeport Mining Company town, Kuala Kencana. My driver heard me complain about the hotel cost and told me that a church member was on vacation and had approved my staying in her one bedroom apartment at no charge.

I really don't know why I hesitated to accept the offer, but I did. My driver daily reminded me until I finally prayed for guidance. Clearly the word of the Lord came to me, "Move." I was not happy about moving. (Of course, my reluctance made no sense!) But learning to obey, even with an ugly attitude, is preferred over disobedience. I moved on Friday afternoon and my attitude affected the energy level of that night's sermon presentation.

Early Sabbath morning, Eddie, my translator, knocked on my door informing me that a tribal war had erupted in Tamika and the Sheraton was locked down, secured by military guns and vehicles. Passage in and out of the hotel was both difficult and dangerous. Guests were confined behind the gated area to the restricted area of the hotel compound.

But at Kuala Kencana, I was free to move about in a full apartment rather than a hotel room and the town center was a pleasant short stroll away.

I was so glad I had obeyed, and my ugly attitude? It was replaced by joyful worship and thanksgiving.

DAY 37

BIBLE TEXT: Exodus 2:10 *And the child grew, and she brought him unto Pharaoh's daughter, and he became her son. And she called his name Moses: and she said, Because I drew him out of the water.*

BIBLE REFERENCES: Exodus 2, 6; Numbers 26

---

*A*t the end of twelve years, Jochebed's son went to Pharaoh's daughter's home, where she named him Moses, *because* [she] *drew him out of the water*. However, during the twelve years Moses lived with his mother, she so strongly instilled in Moses the history of his people and God's promise to send a deliverer that it did not matter that he lived in the palace; Moses knew he would be where God wanted him to be when God called him to higher service. (He just didn't expect it to be forty years later, see Exodus 3.) As Moses studied in the courts of Pharaoh, he wondered how God would free His people. Moses, like Jesus, was twelve when he knew that he would be about God's business.

Jochebed and Hannah took seriously the rearing of their sons for God. Samuel was just a little child when he left his mother to live at the temple in Shiloh, and Moses was young when he entered Pharaoh's palace.

Often parents think their little ones are too young to learn spiritual lessons of life. Parents delay teaching them to pray or to obey because it requires diligent and devoted commitment.

I traveled to the Republic of Panama with a delegation from Tallahassee to promote the importance of civic education in public schools. We were duly impressed with the projects undertaken and successfully completed by elementary and high school students. For them, clean water and drug free parks were a priority as they pushed their public officials to improve the quality of life in their communities.

One of the host team members traveled with her young son. I watched as he asserted himself, defiantly challenging his mother's authority. In anger and frustration, exacerbated by his long overdue missed nap, he went so far as to strike her. I reminded myself that it was not my business to offer any help to the overwhelmed and embarrassed mother. Besides, how would she react to a stranger involving herself in the strictly private matter of discipline between a mother and her child?

As we departed the bus for lunch, I was determined to walk away, but the next thing I knew the little lad was in my arms. With all his might he resisted my firm and solid grip upon his small body. I spoke kindly to him, assuring him that I would not hurt him even though he was striking me. I secured his arms so that they were no longer free to move. The more he resisted being held, the more I increased the intensity of my hold.

He cried louder, expecting his mother to rescue him in just a second. I moved further away from the group and his mother, all the while assuring her that both the situation and her son were okay. The more he resisted my bear hold on his body, the more he exhausted himself until finally he could fight no more and restful sleep quieted him.

Help a mother positively train her child.

RAHAB

DAY 38

BIBLE TEXT: Joshua 2:1 *And Joshua the son of Nun sent out of Shittim two men to spy secretly, saying, Go view the land, even Jericho. And they went, and came into an harlot's house, named Rahab, and lodged there.*

BIBLE REFERENCES: Joshua 2, 6; Matthew 1; Hebrews 11; James 2

---

*R*ahab's story in Joshua 2 and 6 introduces us to a heathen woman who chose to cast her lot with the Israelites, unlike Hagar, who had no choice. Rahab's story occurred after Moses' death when the children of Israel were about to enter the Promised Land. Some forty years earlier, when Moses sent twelve spies to inspect the Promised Land, the people rejected Joshua and Caleb's minority report (Numbers 13).

Now, as the succeeding generations were about to cross Jordan, spies were again sent to inspect Canaan and, in particular, Jericho, a city with double walls and well protected against attacks. Jericho was like the front door to Canaan (Joshua 2).

When the spies arrived in Jericho they stayed at Rahab's motel, which may have been more like a brothel, because it most likely would have aroused little concern or drawn little attention. However, they were noticed and the king sent soldiers to Rahab's inn to arrest the two spies.

What were the best of the church's men doing at a brothel? What would the church folks think when they learned that they were there? We can safely assume that the church folks most likely would not accept that God led them to Rahab's motel. But Rahab's story settles once and for all that the Holy Spirit is available to any and everyone.

We tend to judge others based upon what we can see; thus, we often miss opportunities to share with them our beliefs and testimonies of how God has blessed us. We just assume that because people do not fit within the realm of our expectations of how "seekers" should look, they could not possibly be interested in spiritual matters.

I have a friend with whom I often wondered if and how to share my faith because she seemed so uninterested in spiritual matters. I debated whether to send her a birthday card with a religious theme, but because I was convinced that the Holy Spirit was directing me, I sent it—late! (That confirms how much I struggled with delivering the card.) Her wonderfully positive response to the card confirmed, again, that God does not need me to second guess His directives; obedience is what He desires.

DAY 39

BIBLE TEXT: Joshua 2:4 *And the woman took the two men, and hid them, and said thus, There came men unto me, but I wist not whence they were.*

BIBLE REFERENCES: Joshua 2, 6; Matthew 1; Hebrews 11; James 2

---

*I*t seems almost immediately that the king got word the spies had entered the city "to search out the country" and were staying at Rahab's house that night. The king promptly sent word to Rahab to *Bring forth the men that are come to thee, which are entered into thine house* (Joshua 2:3).

Rahab outright lied! She told the soldiers that the spies were gone, that they probably slipped out the gates before the king ordered the gates closed, and if the soldiers hurried, they might catch them (Joshua 2:5,7). Rahab knew how to keep a straight face and not flinch; she had hidden the spies under a pile of flax drying on her rooftop (Joshua 2:6).

Since the Bible reports events as they happened, Rahab's white lie has been fodder for much discussion and used by many as an explanation for speaking untrue statements to foster the greater good. Did she lie because in her mind it was not a lie, or because she had no morals or scruples against lying? Maybe she knew it was a lie, but under the clear and present danger to the spies, was it a necessary lie?

When we are tempted to lie, the best tactic is to obey the plain word of God, *Thou shall not bear false witness against thy neighbor*

(Exodus 20:16). We are not Rahab nor do we have the ability to judge her lie as God did.

When I was in the first grade, my family lived in a small rural community of Spring Hope, North Carolina. Like most school students, I took a bag lunch to school and had a nickel to buy milk. While I can't remember which one, I longed to have either a hot lunch like a few "privileged" students or a milkshake treat.

Whichever I got, my brother Joseph saw it and immediately upon arriving home asked my Mother why I got a special treat. With eight children, my parents' money was tight and any deviation from the normal allocation was sure to be noticed. I had stolen the quarter from my parents' dresser and promptly lied to my mother about where I had gotten the money.

That experience taught me the implications of Galatians 6:7, *Be not deceived: God is not mocked: for whatsoever a man soweth, that shall he also reap*. My mother seemed less concerned about my stealing than my lying. The corporal punishment I received imprinted permanently in my brain that if I was willing to do wrong, I must be willing to take all of the consequences of the wrong action. I often wonder if I would have been punished for the theft if I had just told the truth.

Do not pile wrong decisions upon bad choices. At all times, in every circumstance, for any reason, and in each situation, we should follow this rule.

DAY 40

BIBLE TEXT: Joshua 2:8, 9 *And before they were laid down, she came up unto them upon the roof; And she said unto the men, I know that the Lord hath given you the land, and that your terror is fallen upon us, and that all the inhabitants of the land faint because of you.*

BIBLE REFERENCES: Joshua 2, 6; Matthew 1; Hebrews 11; James 2

*R*ahab confessed to the spies that everyone in Jericho knew that their God had given Canaan to Israel. Rahab listed the mighty works of God on Israel's behalf. She recounted how Israel walked across the dry Red Sea, but Pharaoh's army drowned; the utter destruction of Sihon, the Amorite king, who refused to let the children of Israel pass through Amorite territory; and how Og, the King of Basham, suffered defeat because he dared to array his forces against God's chosen people (Numbers 21).

Rightly so, Jericho was anxious and afraid; its citizens were filled with dread and fear about their short term future, for *as soon as we had heard these things, our hearts did melt, neither did there remain any more courage in any man, because of you: for the Lord your God, he is God in heaven above, and in earth beneath* (Joshua 2:11).

Their hearts sank and they lost all hope of defeating the Israelites because they knew Israel's Lord was (and is) the Lord of heaven and earth. The citizens of Jericho couldn't even consider that they could be saved, knowing the 100% probability of Jericho's destruction.

Yet, while Rahab's reasoning was based upon sight consistent with what she knew God had done, she was *willing* to make a leap of faith that this same destroying God was a saving God to anyone who believed in Him. That this Jericho harlot would grab hold of faith in the darkest of times is in itself just amazing! How did she know to *be confident of the things we hope for and to be sure of the things we can't see* (Hebrews 11:1)? [iii]

What made Rahab believe in Israel's God? How could she, a heathen, have more faith in God's ability to provide for her than the chosen children of Israel? Was it simply by hearing about what the God of Israel had done?

When did she make the decision to cast her lot with the spies? The Bible doesn't make it sound like there was time for a Bible study or a "come to God" conversation.

Why did Rahab exercise faith in a new and totally different God *who is able to do immeasurably far beyond what we can ask or imagine, and who wants to do even more for us by His power in our lives* (Ephesians 3:20)?

I've heard it said that when we are in heaven, we will find that God had a lot of blessings allocated for us which we did not receive because we never asked for them. Rahab's choice confirms that there is power when we believe, in spite of what we see and in spite of our natural and reasonable fears.

Many of us struggle with faithfulness in returning honest tithes and giving reasonable offerings. Some preachers point out that we trust God with our salvation and to take us to heaven, but not with our monthly expenses. Is there something wrong with that picture?

DAY 41

BIBLE TEXT: Joshua 2:12 *Now therefore, I pray you, swear unto me by the Lord, since I have shewed you kindness, that ye will also shew kindness unto my father's house, and give me a true token.*

BIBLE REFERENCES: Joshua 2, 6; Matthew 1; Hebrews 11; James 2

---

*B*efore Rahab sent the spies safely away, she made them promise her that she and her family would be saved when Jericho was defeated. She knew this would happen because God had already defeated powerful kings on Israel's behalf. Rahab then let the men down the window along the wall with a red rope.

How did Rahab and the spies arrive at their deal to save Rahab and her family when Jericho was captured? Did she hide the spies in exchange for their promised protection or did the spies give her the promise in honor of her protection? That question is rather like asking which was first, the chicken or the egg. The answer depends upon which point in time is used to answer the question.

The motivating factor is really hard to distinguish because the story implies that there was little time for Rahab to scheme and plan, analyze and consider, call a family meeting, or weigh all the options, and then finally come to a well reasoned course of action. Most likely, the outcome would have been eternally different had Rahab taken the time to engage in any of the thoughtful reflections listed above.

Instead, Rahab took two prompt and distinct actions: she showed kindness and she asked for kindness. Her example shows that there are times when, without understanding, we must yield to the directions of our inner voice, the Holy Spirit's guidance. Time is of the essence. God's timing is always right, whether we agree or not.

As we grow in our spiritual maturity, we learn that obedience to the Holy Spirit's leading becomes our most important challenge and obligation.

We show ourselves, others, and God that we love Him by obeying the "still small voice" buried within our hearts (1 Kings 19:12). John declared that *we know that He abideth in us, by the Spirit which He hath given us* (1 John 3:24). But how amazing is God's love for us that even when we did not recognize His leading in our lives, He was leading us, drawing us, and wooing us to Himself.

How often do we hear others' testimonies about how God protected them when they had no idea, concept, or desire to know about the Creator God? They recount stories and experiences, one after another, which make them shudder now as they appreciate the heavenly angels' intense and intensive protective care. Their praise and thanksgiving often turn to tears of joy and worship as they "see" how different their lives would have been but for that one moment in time when they heard and obeyed the Holy Spirit's voice.

When was the last time you shared your testimony?

DAY 42

BIBLE TEXT: Joshua 2:18 *Behold, when we come into the land, thou shalt bind this line of scarlet thread in the window which thou didst let us down by: and thou shalt bring thy father, and thy mother, and thy brethren, and all thy father's household, home unto thee.*

BIBLE REFERENCES: Joshua 2, 6; Matthew 1; Hebrews 11; James 2

---

*T*he spies told Rahab that if she didn't double-cross them and if she marked her house with the red rope in her window when Jericho was defeated, she and all who were in her house would be saved. Suppose Rahab believed that she would be saved when Jericho fell, but had not tied the red rope in the window or had told her family to wait in their own homes.

But Rahab resolved to obey, to simply do as the spies instructed. She didn't modify, change or argue with their explicit directions. Thus, *Joshua had said unto the two men that had spied out the country, Go into the harlot's house, and bring out thence the woman, and all that she hath, as ye sware unto her* (Joshua 6:22).

Because she did as the spies instructed, it was easy for the spies to find her house. *And Joshua saved Rahab the harlot alive, and her father's household, and all that she had; and she dwelleth in Israel even unto this day; because she hid the messengers, which Joshua sent to spy out Jericho* (Joshua 6:25).

Rahab obeyed the last instructions given!

Rahab's story settles once and for all that faith without works is dead (James 2:20, 26). Faith requires work or action, even if it is "standing still and waiting for the salvation of the Lord" (Exodus 14:13). But sometimes we get works confused with salvation. The Bible is clear. Our salvation is "the gift of God" (Eph. 2:8). So that's not the issue!

The issue is, "What happens next?" According to Philippians 1:6 and 2:5, we must allow the work God began in us to continue as we grow up and mature into having a mind like Christ.

A baby has nothing to do with its birth. But as it lives, it grows from being fed and changed to feeding itself and being potty trained. If babies do not achieve predictable milestones, then parents become anxious and consult doctors.

So it is in our Christian experience. We climb Peter's ladder by adding to our faith virtue, knowledge, temperance, then patience, godliness, brotherly kindness, and charity (2 Peter 1:5-8).

When I was a child, my parents took us on vacations to New York, and because there were ten of us we traveled in two cars. My father was in the lead car, giving directions to my brothers who were driving.

We were from Greensboro, North Carolina, so New York was big and unfamiliar to us. After my brothers had driven for what seemed like hours, they would ask my father for confirmation of the directions. My father would reply, "Follow the last directions given!"

Each time we obey the last instruction given, God gives us more instructions, until we, like Enoch, become so in sync with His will that when we are doing our own will, we are obeying God's will for our lives.

DAY 43

BIBLE TEXT: Matthew 1:5 *Salmon begat Boaz of Rachab; and Boaz begat Obed of Ruth: and Obed begat Jesse. And Jesse begat David the king.*

BIBLE REFERENCES: Joshua 2, 6; Matthew 1; Hebrews 11; James 2

---

*R*ahab became King David's great-great-grandmother. When she was safely with the children of Israel, Rahab married and became the mother of Boaz, who married Ruth. They were the parents of Obed, who was the father of Jesse, the father of David, from whom Jesus descended. Not bad for a prostitute!

Her story confirms that we cannot predict what God will do with our lives when we submit to His will. (So it is best that we not try to weed out folks for His kingdom.) There was absolutely no way Rahab could know the eternal purposes God had for her. She was not there when Moses outlined for Israel the blessings and curses which were the consequences of choosing obedience or disobedience to God's way (Deuteronomy 28).

Rahab could not know that her decision to believe and her resolve to obey would result in such eternal rewards. God's favor was beyond her wildest imagination. *Eye hath not seen, nor ears heard, neither have entered into the hearts of man, the things which God has prepared for them that love Him* (1 Corinthians 2:9).

Rahab's story stresses the importance of sharing the good news with others. The measure of our influence will only be understood in the earth made new because only there will we see the results of loving words and deeds performed in honor of our relationship with Jesus (Matthew 25:31-46).

Fortunately, we don't have to wait until heaven for God's rewards. Today, God rewards us beyond our wildest imaginations. Like Rahab, we testify that it is really true, *Eye hath not seen, nor ears heard, neither have entered into the hearts of man, the things which God has prepared for them that love Him* (1 Corinthians 2:9).

Studying God's names tells us something about His character. The very first time I heard the song, "More Than Enough,"[iv] tears welled up in my eyes as I played it over and over again. I researched the origin of the song and discovered my response was identical to that of others upon their hearing it for the first time.

> Jehovah Jireh, my provider, You are more than enough for me.
> Jehovah Raphe, You're my healer, by Your stripes I have been
>   set free.
> Jehovah Shammah, You are with me, to supply all my needs,
> You're more than enough, Lord, You're more than enough,
> You are more than enough for me.

I have come to understand that Jehovah Jireh means more than "my provider." It means that before I know that I need it, God has already provided it for me.

DAY 44

BIBLE TEXT: Hebrews 11:31 *By faith the harlot Rahab perished not with them that believed not, when she had received the spies with peace.*

BIBLE REFERENCES: Joshua 2, 6; Matthew 1; Hebrews 11; James 2

---

*O*nly two women are listed in Paul's roll call of the faithful and Rahab is one of them. Those listed share in common a life changing moment when, without possessing the promise, they believed it as true, embraced it, confessed it, and engaged all of their energies to move toward it. John the Revelator confirms that those outside the walls of the New Jerusalem will include the "unbelieving" (Revelation 21:8).

Faith is easy to talk about but very hard to practice. In my house is a painted decorative sign, "Faith is believing when it is beyond the power of reason to believe." Everything in Jericho was destroyed except Rahab and all those in her house, and the silver, gold, and vessels of brass and iron which were saved for the treasury of the Lord (Joshua 6).

Faith, by definition, requires us to march to the beat of a different drummer, to travel unknown and unfamiliar paths, to go where none have gone before. Faith includes standing apart, standing against, standing by, standing despite, standing for, standing outside, standing out, standing through, standing until, standing up, standing by yourself, just you—standing (Ephesians 6:13). And even if others stand with you, their presence cannot dilute your commitment and passion. Remember Lot's wife (Genesis 19).

The people of Jericho were judged and destroyed because of their sins. Rahab's story demonstrates that God will utterly destroy the wicked and the unbelieving. Anyone who chooses to classify himself or herself as wicked or unbelieving will be destroyed, and that even includes some church people today, as it did among "the chosen" in Bible days.

God's "strange work, strange act" is the final destruction of the wicked, which brings about the ultimate end of sin and sinners (Matthew 13:40; Isaiah 28:21). Everyone receives the consequences of his or her choices, some to "life eternal" and others to "everlasting punishment" (Matthew 25:46).

My job as a judge includes determining and dispensing just consequences to defendants who chose to disobey the law. While I may be kind and compassionate, nevertheless, I dispense punishment as well as judgment. The citizens of Leon County, Florida, expect me to do my job.

Why do we expect anything less of the Judge of the Universe?

DAY 45

BIBLE TEXT: James 2:25 *Likewise also was not Rahab the harlot justified by works, when she had received the messengers, and had sent them out another way?*

BIBLE REFERENCES: Joshua 2, 6; Matthew 1; Hebrews 11; James 2

James says Rahab's "walk matched her talk." She was justified, moving from death to life, and her character transformed because she did something based upon and in light of her faith. God promises that *whosoever believeth on Him shall have everlasting life* (John 3:16). *Faith without works is dead* (James 2:20).

Rahab's story gives us hope; God can and will change us from nothing to something of value. Paul explained to Timothy that some vessels are for serving fine dinners, while other vessels are for everyday use or trash disposal (2 Timothy 2:20, 21). Every vessel is *not* a vessel of honor. Clay and ceramic vessels are not golden vessels. But if "vessel" is analogized with character, then Rahab's story totally changes the image of a vessel's use. An ordinary clay pot can become a highly valued vessel of great worth and significance, a chosen vessel. How?

When we allow Jesus into our hearts, He gives us the gift of the Holy Spirit, who empowers us to be in this world but not of it, *by the renewing of our minds in the perfect will of God* (Romans 12:2). Everything changes when Jesus' love permeates our thoughts; it changes our paradigm of life, and thus, our actions. As the old saying goes, "We may not be all that we want to be, but praise God, we are not what we used to be." Our lives bear heavenly fruit of the Spirit: *love, joy, peace, longsuffering, gentleness, goodness, faith, meekness, temperance, righteousness, and truth* (Galatians 5:22, 23; Ephesians 5:9).

The faith and works discussion really is quite simple. Our lives constantly illustrate the correlation between the two. When we want something and believe we can "get" it, we roll up our sleeves and work for it! We tell our children that we believe they can do better, they then believe that they can do better, and then they work to do better. Likewise, good teachers, coaches, and bosses motivate students and workers to stretch themselves to do better work and become better people.

When we believe that the Holy Spirit helps us to become more like the character of Christ, we are willing to work with Him as He helps us bring *into captivity every thought to the obedience of Christ* (2 Corinthians 10:5). We do not serve God to be saved. We are saved upon confessing Christ as the *Lamb of God, which taketh away the sin of the world* (John 1:29). We serve God because we are saved. So we act like saved people who have the desire to fully and correctly model the life of Christ Jesus (Philippians 2:5).

What did you do in the last twenty-four hours which was an "act of faith"?

ZELOPHEHAD'S DAUGHTERS

DAY 46

BIBLE TEXT: Numbers 26:33 *And Zelophehad the son of Hepher had no sons, but daughters: and the names of the daughters of Zelophehad were Mahlah, and Noah, Hoglah, Milcah, and Tirzah.*

BIBLE REFERENCES: Numbers 26, 27, 36; Joshua 17; 1 Chronicles 7

---

*I*t is always impressive when one is remembered by name, and in Bible days when a woman's name was recorded, it flagged a point worthy of pause, attention, and study. Thus, we meet the five daughters of Zelophehad, a fifth generation descendant of Joseph. Joseph, Jacob's favorite son, had two sons, one of whom was Manasseh. Manassah's son was Makir, whose son was Gilead; Gilead's son was Hepher, and his son was Zelophehad. Zelophehad had only daughters: Mahlah, Noah, Hoglah, Milcah, and Tirzah (Numbers 26).

God includes women in "His-story" of history. Women matter to God. No cultures, customs, practices, traditions, heritages, habits, or conveniences can supersede or diminish God's value for each person God Himself made and fashioned with His own hands (Psalm 119:73). In Psalm 139:14, David exclaims that humankind is *fearfully and wonderfully made*. God knows that His thoughts toward us are of *peace and not of evil, to give* [us] *a future and a hope* (Jeremiah 29:11, NJKV). Solomon's description of virtuous women in Proverbs 31 paints a word picture of God's image of His chosen daughters, women who "fear the Lord."

Women were an integral part of the Messiah's mission. He valued them as more than just housekeepers, mothers, caregivers, and workers. They were eyewitnesses to His ministry; they testified of His power, were recipients of His miracles, and confirmed His gracious grace and abundant mercy. Women participated in spreading the good news of the Gospel, introduced others to Jesus, provided for His earthly needs, and supported the cause of Christ with their resources.

When God esteems women so highly, should we do less? We must diligently fight against and strive to prevent our cultures, customs, practices, traditions, heritages, habits, or conveniences from defining and limiting our understanding of God's value of women.

DAY 47

BIBLE TEXT: Numbers 27:1, 2 *Then came the daughters of Zelophehad . . . And they stood before Moses, and before Eleazar the priest, and before the princes and all the congregation, by the door of the tabernacle of the congregation . . .*

BIBLE REFERENCES: Numbers 26, 27, 36; Joshua 17; 1 Chronicles 7

*T*his text begins by explaining why these five sisters' names were recorded in Bible history. United, they came to the entrance of the tabernacle, seeking their audience with Moses, the busy leader of the children of Israel. Without embarrassment or hesitation, they stood in the presence of the priest, the princes, and the entire congregation. These sisters demonstrated courage—extraordinary courage, passion, and commitment. Their boldness established the precedent for Queen Esther, who would later come before King Ahasuerus (Esther 5).

There is no other record of women approaching Moses with their concerns during the wilderness experience; thus, we can assume that women's positions and contributions were directly linked to their fathers, husbands, or brothers. Whatever a woman needed or wanted, it was channeled through a man. What these five sisters did was unprecedented, unheard of. It was just not done.

There is an old saying, "Nothing ventured, nothing gained." How often do we miss opportunities of change because we lack courage, passion, and commitment? When we consider the obstacles in our way and the difficulties looming before us, our hearts faint before we even begin to tackle the task. It seems that everyone in our sphere of influence speaks words of discouragement, accurately pointing out the impossibilities and graphically painting pictures of defeat. Maybe we should not consult with those who have dim eyes of faith.

Accomplishments and successes begin with an idea, a mental reality that what is not can actually be, so the clearer the vision, the more diligent the effort to turn the idea into physical reality. The mental image takes on life-giving properties, self-fulfilling qualities, and self-actualization abilities. While it may be difficult to put into words the energy ideas create, everyone who has ever experienced an idea becoming reality shares a common moment of "It is done!"

My first mission trip began as an idea to give God a special thank you gift for 50 years of life. As I sought the appropriate gift, my energy and enthusiasm grew until finally, the idea turned into a plan. The plan of giving the gift of my time, combined with my love of travel, yielded commitment to share the gospel in foreign lands.

DAY 48

BIBLE TEXT: Numbers 27:4 *Why should the name of our father be done away from among his family, because he hath no son? Give unto us therefore a possession among the brethren of our father.*

BIBLE REFERENCES: Numbers 26, 27, 36; Joshua 17; 1 Chronicles 7

---

*W*hy had the sisters balked at tradition, rejected custom, and ignored practice to seek an audience with Moses, and done so in the presence of all the people? They demanded to be treated equally with sons for inheritance purposes. The sisters' assertion for equal treatment alongside sons was a bold demand. What the sisters requested was revolutionary!

Zelophehad's daughters argued that their father did not participate in Korah's rebellion. Why the sisters referred to this particular incident is not clear. There were many examples of rebellion to which they could have alluded. Maybe there had been wide spread support for Korah, and the sisters wanted to highlight their father's loyalty to God.

Numbers 16 records the rebellion of Korah and his 250 men of renown. They also stood at the door of the tabernacle when they challenged Moses and Aaron's divine calling as the leaders of the children of Israel. God confirmed that He had chosen Moses and Aaron when Korah died an unnatural death as the earth opened up and swallowed him, his family and their houses and everything that pertained to them. The leading 250 men were consumed by fire. It settled and answered any questions about whether Aaron's seed was ordained as the priests of Israel.

Maybe the sisters chose Korah's rebellion to show that there was no reason why their father would have been denied an allotment of land. Or maybe the sisters were confirming that their father's bloodline continued after the rebellion.

They also argued that their father died in the wilderness according to God's punishment against all the Israelites who were over twenty years of age because they accepted the false spies' report (Numbers 14). Therefore, they concluded, there was no basis upon which they should be denied land just because their father had no sons.

Their demand stunned Moses, all of the men, and all of the people. Radical change usually stuns those in leadership positions.

DAY 49

BIBLE TEXT: Numbers 27:7 *The daughters of Zelophehad speak right: thou shalt surely give them a possession of an inheritance among their father's brethren; and thou shalt cause the inheritance of their father to pass unto them.*

BIBLE REFERENCES: Numbers 26, 27, 36; Joshua 17; 1 Chronicles 7

---

*S*urely, many fathers had died without a son, so the issue of daughters inheriting must have been discussed prior to Zelophehad's death. But the Bible records that Moses did not know how to respond to Zelophehad's daughters, so he *brought their cause before the Lord* (Numbers 27:5). Chances are no one, except the sisters, was ready for God's response. He agreed with them!

God said, *If a man die, and have no son, then ye shall cause his inheritance to pass unto his daughter* (Numbers 27:8). God established the precedent of equal treatment of sons and daughters for inheritance purposes; thus, the sisters' story is repeated in Joshua 17 and 1 Chronicles 7.

Interestingly, in the book of Job, whose story is thought to have occurred prior to the Exodus, it is recorded that Job *gave* [his daughters] *inheritance among their brethren* (Job 42:15). Maybe the sisters knew about Job's daughters' equal standing. Today, every state has intestate laws which determine inheritance, and probably, all states treat sons and daughters equally.

Too often we have not because we ask not (James 4:2). Fear of failure acts like a stun gun—we are paralyzed, unable to take any steps toward our dreams and desires. We can see them, but we are afraid to grab hold of them.

At 31 years old, I enrolled in law school. Granted, I had gotten a shove from my immediate supervisor when she shared her opinion with me that I was not measuring up to her expectation of how I should perform my job. Her box was not a good fit for me. But I still had a choice to make. Would I leave the security of my job and go where I had no experience or roadmap or even a point of reference? There were no attorneys in my family. I probably did not have enough sense to be scared of failure and sometimes that is a good thing!

After two years in a small law firm, I hung out my own shingle. Again, I probably did not have enough sense to be scared of failure. Then I ran for county judge in 1996. Surely, I did not have enough sense to be scared of failure.

Somewhere along the way, the image of Peter walking on the water bore itself into my spirit (Matthew 14). He answered his own question by taking a step of faith. Too often we focus on the rest of Peter's experience, drawing many appropriate applications, but the fact still remains that Peter is the only person to walk on water. In the power of Jesus' invitation, Peter left the boat, all his security, and began his journey toward the Savior.

Like Zelophehad's daughters and Peter, we must do something that moves us toward our goals, dreams, and desires. A step of faith is, more often times than not, rewarded with a road to success.

DAY 50

BIBLE TEXT: Numbers 36:6 *This is the thing which the Lord doth command concerning the daughters of Zelophehad, saying, Let them marry to whom they think best; only to the family of the tribe of their father shall they marry.*

BIBLE REFERENCES: Numbers 26, 27, 36; Joshua 17; 1 Chronicles 7

---

*T*he contribution of Zelophehad's daughters impacted the history of the children of Israel. Were Moses and the people ready to fully accept God's response to the daughters' demand since the inheritance was land? Keeping the tribe's land within the tribe was paramount, so God added the limitation about who the sisters could marry to prevent confusion. The daughters were commanded to marry within the tribe to ensure that land did not pass outside of the tribe. With this proviso, the division of the Promised Land would account for daughters who had no brothers. Additionally, the limitation upon the daughters protected the family tribal line, which was also an important concern and goal.

God values women and the sisters' demand afforded Him circumstances to re-affirm women's rights to justice and fairness under His order of things.

However, the book of Job poses an interesting question. If the book of Job is the first book of human history, representing a time prior to the history of Abraham, then women's inheritance rights were already clearly established, *And in all the land were no women found so fair as the daughters of Job: and their father gave them inheritance among their brethren* (Job 42:15). How then did women lose the right of inheritance?

Could it be that a consequence of the intermarriages of the "sons of God" with the daughters of the "sons of men" (Genesis 6) fostered devaluation of women? Eve's punishment for sin required that [her] *desire shall be to* [her] *husband, and he shall rule over* [her] (Genesis 3:16). But it did not change the fact that Eve was created equal to, but different from Adam.

Under the guise of whatever theory justifies their actions, men's superiority is attained at the expense of women. And, too often, it is women who support male domination because women do not appreciate that God created them equal to, but different from men. Only heaven has a complete record of the pain, anguish, hurt, and evil men have done to women simply because they were women.

During my teaching experiences, I have encountered students whose physical appearances could at best be described as leaving a little (or a lot) to be desired. How quickly and easily we judge a person's character by outward appearances. I remember a young girl whose face was marred by protruding eyes, but as I interacted with her, I found her to be lovely in character, intelligent, and of excellent attitude. It dawned on me one day that I no longer saw the wrapping because the gift was so beautiful.

We all descended from Adam and Eve, who were fashioned by

the hand of God. Each human is divinely gifted and all the gifts are needed and necessary. Does it really matter if the gift holder is male or female?

Why?

WOMAN WITH AN ISSUE OF BLOOD

DAY 51

BIBLE TEXT: Mark 5:25 *And a certain woman, which had an issue of blood twelve years.*

BIBLE REFERENCES: Matthew 9; Mark 5; Luke 8

---

*A*dditional information disclosed Jochebed's name, but not so with this woman. Even though her story is told by three Bible writers, we never learn this woman's name; she was simply known by her diseased condition, i.e., "an issue of blood." Mark added that she was "a certain woman."

The three gospel writers present the events differently; Matthew simply recorded that it occurred. To him, she was just a woman, labeled by her disease, who interrupted Jesus' travel to Jarius' house in response to his plea to heal his 12 year-old daughter. Matthew's account seems to imply that he was annoyed that she interfered with Jesus' main purpose and mission of helping Jarius, a ruler of the synagogue. Jarius was an important person and man, whose request on behalf of his daughter was worthy of immediate attention from Jesus.

But the woman had no man to intercede on her behalf. She was a nobody, nameless, and unworthy of attention or value because she could not meet society's expectations as a wife, mother, caregiver, household manager, or market place entrepreneur. To those around her, she was a marginalized person. Her bloody condition made her ritually unclean (religious isolation), interfered with her contact with others (social isolation), and the condition was a great source of discomfort and inconvenience (physical isolation). Most likely, the woman saw herself as everyone else saw her, and the emotional isolation stripped her of hope and self-dignity.

Sometimes it is really hard to know which isolation is the hardest to bear; if refuted, which isolation would change the outcome of any person's situation and circumstances.

My involvement with issues related to domestic violence has exposed me to a key factor explaining why victims are victims. Domestic violence can only exist as batterers isolate their victims. Statistics verify that females are overwhelmingly the victims, and research confirms that abusive men gain control by exerting behaviors designed to isolate and undermine the victims' self-image and self-worth. These relationships thrive as the couples closely guard their secrets, which promotes isolation and prevents exposure to others' evaluation of the couples' experiences. They accept abusive experiences as their norm, rather than seeing them as the abnormal, toxic, and dangerous events they are.

As long as victims see themselves reflected in the batterers' eyes, there is no chance for change; no chance for hope.

DAY 52

BIBLE TEXT: Mark 5:26 *And had suffered many things of many physicians, and had spent all that she had, and was nothing bettered, but rather grew worse.*

BIBLE REFERENCES: Matthew 9; Mark 5; Luke 8

---

*M*ark's account shared that the doctors could not help this "certain woman" with "an issue of blood." She had spent all her resources, "all of her living," Dr. Luke wrote, without any relief. The woman had earlier been a woman of value and worth to her family and friends; she most likely had a husband who loved her and willingly paid for her medical treatments. Her family was supportive and encouraging. They had hoped that a cure was available. Surely there was a doctor who knew what to do.

But the doctors' appointments continued and the days turned into months and the months into years. For twelve long years she had suffered without relief and cure. She grew worse. Probably, even if she wanted to see another doctor, she was without resources to do so. Her condition made it impossible for her to work. Whatever family support she had was now gone. She was a drain upon the family's resources and she was outliving her financial resources.

She had reached the place where there was no reason to expect anything more than a life confined to physical pain, social segregation, religious rejection, and emotional isolation. Her only question was, "How long before death finally releases me from this hopeless and impossible situation?"

American culture is confronting the new phenomenon of the elderly living longer and longer. Medical science and technology have extended life expectancy. Better lifestyles and healthier choices are ensuring people against early death from avoidable diseases. The Bible's *threescore and ten, and if by reason of strength they be fourscore years* (Psalm 90:10) is now normal. Many persons live well into their 90s and some celebrate 100th birthdays.

Unlike many other cultures, Americans put their senior citizens in assisted living and nursing homes. Families are often legitimately unable, or selfishly unwilling, to live in a multi-generational setting. Emotional and financial resources are taxed heavily to care for an aged loved one. There has probably always been the "sandwiched generation," i.e., people caring for aged parents and children at the same time, but it seems more stressful and disruptive today.

Based upon their families' behavior, seniors often rightly conclude that they are burdens and "in the way." Like the woman who had an issue of blood, they are confined to lives of physical pain, social segregation, religious rejection, and emotional isolation.

DAY 53

BIBLE TEXT: Mark 5:27 *When she had heard of Jesus, came in the press behind, and touched his garment.*

BIBLE REFERENCES: Matthew 9; Mark 5; Luke 8

---

*O*nly Mark added this insight about the bloody woman's experience. In the shortest Gospel, Mark focused upon what Jesus did—His miracles. Mark's writing style is pregnant with action and vivid descriptions.

When she heard of Jesus! Pause, stop, and reflect a moment. Let your mind imagine and heart feel the impact of those words. *When she heard of Jesus* her paradigm changed. Her heart leaped at the chance to see Jesus. Her mind determined to find this Jesus. Her will gathered itself together to push her one more time to seek help for her issue of blood. Hope shoved despair back. Mercy hurtled medical opinions to the side. Love propelled doubt out of the way! She had heard of Jesus!

Hearing of Jesus has the same effect as putting dry seeds into the soil. The apparently lifeless seed, when connected to the soil, water, and sunlight, finds life within itself, then sprouts, and becomes a strong plant, even an oak tree from an acorn.

Maybe it was easy for Mark to include information about the woman's mental state since Mark himself had experienced a paradigm shift in his mental state. Mark quit and returned home during his first mission trip with Paul and Barnabas, which caused such a dispute between them that they decided to go their separate ways (Acts 15). But eventually, Mark "heard of Jesus" and what a change was wrought in him. Paul wrote in 2 Timothy 4:11 that Mark was *profitable to me for the ministry.*

When we heard from the doctor at Mayo Clinic about a new drug which might "cure" Jason's Crohn's disease, hope sprung up in our hearts that finally he could have non-surgical relief. The fact that the drug was expensive was not a concern. His father, Jim, said that he was willing to do whatever it took for "his boy" to have the three treatments. Only the doctor's insistence that we try to obtain prior insurance coverage approval delayed the first treatment. (Good thing, because it was approved, it was expensive, and it worked.)

Lives are changed when people hear of Jesus! Two of my good friends were invited to an old fashioned evangelistic tent meeting. Their marriage was in dire straits because of alcohol abuse and related issues. But on the very first night the husband sat in the audience, he heard of Jesus. Hope sprung up in his heart that change was not just possible, but for real. All of his grandmother's prayers were answered and translated into action as he accepted Christ as his personal Savior.

His life has never been the same.

DAY 54

BIBLE TEXT: Mark 5:28 *For she said, If I may touch but his clothes, I shall be whole.*

BIBLE REFERENCES: Matthew 9; Mark 5; Luke 8

---

*T*he woman with an issue of blood came behind Jesus, pressing her way through the crowd to touch the hem of His garment. Unlike Jarius, who had talked to Jesus face to face with the disciples' approval and support, she felt powerless, unimportant, and unworthy of Jesus' time and attention. She also knew that the disciples would not be sympathetic; most likely they would intentionally block her access to Jesus. After all, she was a woman with an issue of blood!

There were historical and current examples in support of the woman believing there was healing power in the hem of Jesus' robe. During their wilderness journey from Egypt to Canaan, God sent fiery serpents in response to Israel's complaints against Moses. When they confessed that their sin was against God, He instructed Moses to make a "serpent of brass, and put it upon a pole," where all who were bitten could look and be healed (Numbers 21). Matthew 14 records that after Jesus fed the 5000 men plus women and children, He quieted the winds on the Lake of Galilee and saved drowning Peter. When Jesus arrived in Gennersaret, the people gathered all the sick, who *besought* [Jesus] *that they might only touch the hem of his garment: and as many as touched were made perfectly whole* (Mark. 5:36).

What is the equivalent of such faith in today's society? When we hear the testimony of someone who has the bleeding woman's level of faith, it seems incredulous. The person is more often than not dismissed as a bit "touched." How interesting that we should describe the person as "touched" for that is exactly what happened; they also, like the woman with an issue of blood, touched in faith the hem of Jesus' garment!

In my early years in Tallahassee, there was a church member who shared testimonies about how God intervened in her life. She would go up to gas station attendants and say that God had directed her to tell them that they were to give her free gas. She would begin trips which, according to my way of thinking, were poorly planned at best and just downright presumptuous at worst. She would get on the road without money and in cars which were in need of significant repairs. As she shared her stories, I found it just impossible to "wrap my mind around" her experiences until finally the Holy Spirit revealed to me that He is very specific in His approaches to each person.

At that time, in my spiritual state I could not see any sense in her decisions. While I cannot say that I understand her stories any better today, I can say that I do not find them as annoying and neither am I as distrustful. Why? It is okay with me for God to speak to others in their language. It simply requires me to spend more time practicing my language and communication styles with Him.

But I do wonder what blessings have I lost because my faith would not let me believe that there was healing in the hem of Jesus' robe?

DAY 55

BIBLE TEXT: Mark 5:29 *And straightway the fountain of her blood was dried up; and she felt in her body that she was healed of that plague.*

BIBLE REFERENCES: Matthew 9; Mark 5; Luke 8

---

*M*ark says "straightway"; Luke says "immediately." Other versions and translations describe her healing as "at once,"[v] "as soon as,"[vi] "right away,"[vii] "instantly stopped,"[viii] and "moment she did."[ix] It is abundantly clear that while she was touching the hem of Jesus' robe, the woman with an issue of blood was healed. It was instantaneous! As Jesus' healing power surged through her body, *she felt in her body that she was healed of that plague.* She knew she was healed. There was no need for any follow-up visits with any more doctors.

Matthew recorded at least three times that Jesus healed all those who gathered around Him seeking healing. (Matthew 12:15; 14:14; and 15:30). Yet in His hometown of Nazareth, except for a "few folks," *He did not many mighty works there because of their unbelief* (Mark 6:5; Matthew 13:58). Twice, the people of Nazareth rejected Jesus. The woman with the issue of blood was healed during Jesus' second Galilean tour, between the two rejections. Sometimes it is a good thing to be in the crowd, but not of the crowd.

Out of jealousy, did the doctors join forces with the priests and leaders to destroy Jesus' ministry? Jesus healed people of any and every kind of illness, and He did not charge for His services.

Why are not all of God's answers to our prayers "immediate"? Our prayers are often layered with demands that God must do something right now, right away. Why must we wait, even until eternity, for some of the answers to our petitions? This question often causes us to stop praying for we sense that our prayers are not important to God, or we simply give up hope in praying because within our determination of reasonable time, God has not answered.

Ever thought of the word "orchestrate" when considering God's answering of prayers? The Cambridge Advanced Learner's Dictionary On-Line[x] defines "orchestrate" as "to arrange something carefully, and sometimes unfairly, so as to achieve a desired result."

Some Bible writers imply that the woman with the issue of blood had tried other times to make contact with Jesus; but, in God's infinite wisdom and purpose, it was necessary that her appointment time be that day. We can think of many reasons why, including that the impact of her healing would be more miraculous, surely noted and recorded by the Gospel writers. And, the encounter was an excellent opportunity for the lessons Jesus wanted to teach.

Nothing just happens with God. Everything, even the answer to our prayers, is orchestrated by God for maximum results according to His omnipotent will.

DAY 56

BIBLE TEXT: Mark 5:30 *And Jesus, immediately knowing in himself that virtue had gone out of him, turned him about in the press, and said, Who touched my clothes?*

BIBLE REFERENCES: Matthew 9; Mark 5; Luke 8

Jesus demanded to know, "Who touched me?" Luke recorded that Peter (is it *always* Peter?) questioned Jesus' logic in asking, *Who touched my clothes*? Jesus knew that someone had touched Him because He sensed that *virtue had gone out of him*. Jesus perceived the exercise of His healing power. While it was not a drawdown of His power, did the woman with an issue of blood really think that her draw upon Jesus' healing power would not be noticed by Jesus?

Many had been healed by touching Jesus' clothes, so there was no reason for her to think that her plan would be noticed. She concluded that her well-thought-out plan required her to touch only the very edge of the hem of His garment; she did not need more than that. Even if she thought for a moment that Jesus would know that she had touched Him, her image of herself assured her that He would not take the time to address her—she was a nobody. Peter's question to Jesus confirmed her analysis; her reasoning was correct, except it did not factor in Jesus' response.

Jesus' inquiry revealed that no one and nothing escapes His

notice. He is always aware, always alert, always in tune to anyone's plan to draw virtue from Him.

Ever felt a small insect or bug crawling on your skin? When we are in an area where we expect to find bugs, we are on heightened vigilance and care. We might even sense a bug when there isn't one. On my mission trips to areas where malaria is rampant, I feel mosquitoes which are not there! How sensitive is our sense of touch.

Masterful pickpockets are even able to slip and slide wallets out of buttoned back or front inside pockets without the victim's least bit of awareness. Thus, travelers must take extra precautions when visiting high pickpocket areas.

Attuned parents can sense the presence of their children in their sleep. Healthy hugs are good for the soul, and an encouraging hand on the shoulder lifts spirits and shares burdens. I like to go to sleep at night touching my husband's feet.

The gift of touch and sense of feeling are wonderful blessings. Touch someone today—virtue might flow from you.

DAY 57

BIBLE TEXT: Luke 8:47 *And when the woman saw that she was not hid, she came trembling, and falling down before him.*

BIBLE REFERENCES: Matthew 9; Mark 5; Luke 8

---

*A*s the woman with the issue of blood pressed her way through the multitude, her plans were her secret—until Jesus called her out. *When the woman saw that she was not hid,* she responded to Jesus' question. She knew that Jesus knew. No one else knew, but He did. Neither the size of the crowd, nor her immediate retreat into the crowd was sufficient to conceal her. Because there was healing in His garment, surely He had knowledge of when and who touched His robe. Hidden from Jesus? Never is that an accurate assessment of Jesus' wisdom and power, or our place of being.

With trembling limbs, the healed woman bowed before Jesus. Fear consumed the healed woman—fear of what? Why would Jesus stop the entire procession to find out who had touched just the border of His garment? Would Jesus take back her healing? Would Jesus embarrass her? Would Jesus make a joke of her? Many had touched Jesus before, so why was it necessary to find out who had touched Him this time?

Both Mark and Luke reported that when she came out of the crowd, she fell down at His feet. Notice that Jarius also fell at Jesus' feet when he besought Him to come to his house (Mark 5:22 and

Luke 8:41). Jesus transformed her impersonal touch of His robe into her personal encounter with Him.

When Jesus calls us out from the crowd, like this "certain woman with an issue of blood," we fall at His feet in honest worship and praise. We do not care who sees or knows, our business isn't private anymore. Because of what is occurring in our interchange with Jesus, "It's personal."

Is there a challenge which has too long consumed your time and energy? Be honest about it—name it right now. Jesus knows we need help, but He needs us to disclose it. What is it? Family issues, job related frustrations, financial battles, personality flaws, medical conditions, Christian growth struggles, or insecurities? Just tell Jesus all about it—now.

DAY 58

BIBLE TEXT: Luke 8:47 . . . *She declared unto him before all the people for what cause she had touched him, and how she was healed immediately.*

BIBLE REFERENCES: Matthew 9; Mark 5; Luke 8

S he blurted out her story. With trembling tongues, but gladdened hearts, we too share our story because *it is our* story—"It's personal." At His feet, she was so focused on His compassionate face filled with love, acceptance, and mercy that her story rolled off her tongue: twelve long years of misery and isolation, endless rounds of doctors' appointments, and total consumption of her financial resources. Even though she had lost hope, the seed of faith was planted because she had heard of the man called Jesus, who was passing her way that day. She told Him that she knew that day was *the* day for her healing, and nothing would deprive her of her opportunity.

In her one-on-one interview with Jesus, she was so focused until, like Hannah in the temple, she lost interest in, was unaware of, and unconcerned about the crowd's knowing and seeing her business. At that moment, it was personal between the woman and Jesus.

She testified of her instantaneous, immediate, and straightway healing. Her disease was cured; it was no more! No more misery and isolation; no more endless rounds of doctors' appointments; and no more spending money for doctors' bills. Hope and the seed of faith planted in her dry heart had been watered by the Living Water Himself.

The crowd stood in awed reverence and respect for Jesus. They wondered how could He do such things? Why hadn't they pressed through the crowd for healing of their own maladies?

Like this woman, when Jesus calls us out, we fall at His feet, telling Jesus why we needed His touch. We can't keep it to ourselves; our testimony is demanded. The honesty of our confession connects with the woman's experience.

While we may receive our blessings in secret, there is no shame in admitting that we are at the end of our rope and resources. He requires that we openly confess to Him our needs and that our lives are in shambles. We acknowledge that all our other efforts and attempts have failed. We are sick and tired of being sick and tired.

I had the privilege to perform the wedding of the daughter of a man who was one of the first defendants I sent to jail as a new judge. He was an alcoholic and had several DUIs. Why his new DUI was charged as a misdemeanor was beyond me. A year in jail was all the jail time I could impose.

During my re-election campaign in 2000, I heard from the man's wife. She told me that her husband was a recovered alcoholic and a leader in AA. She told how the disposition I gave her husband was the one which finally worked. Her family was a family once again. What a blessing that was because he was there for her when she faced her bout with cancer.

God ordained that I should be his judge. In his sentence, he saw a chance to recover. With everything in him, he reached out in faith that this time would be the time he could conquer the disease which had plagued his life.

Praise God!

DAY 59

BIBLE TEXT: Mark 5:34 *And he said unto her, Daughter, thy faith hath made thee whole.*

BIBLE REFERENCES: Matthew 9; Mark 5; Luke 8

---

*T*he woman with an issue of blood pushed her faith beyond its limits. Faith, Jesus said, was the healing portion. It has been said that, "Faith is believing when it is beyond the power of reason to believe." Those who grow faith by taking action, expecting results beyond what is humanly possible, are big risk takers. God encourages us to exercise faith. He rewards our efforts to practice and exert faith in the promises found in His Word.

Surely there were others in the crowd who, if they had pressed on and persevered in spite of every sign of apparent defeat, would also have experienced healing. Having a need is not enough; the woman's story teaches that only those who seek relief at all costs will find it. It is only those who against hope, believe in hope, and obtain hope (Romans 4:18). *Faith without works is dead* (James 2:20).

Paul sums up his roll call of the faithful in Hebrews 11:6, *Without faith it is impossible to please Him; for* [s]*he that cometh to God must believe that He is, and that He is a rewarder of them that diligently seek Him.* The faithful in Paul's list accomplished great feats for God because they were willing to take risks even if it meant that others would label them as fanatical or unreasonable. Yet it is our individual faith walk that God wants us to share. People can argue logic, reason, and perceptions, but what we believe about what God has done for us is what we believe.

That is why we can all share our own story of how Jesus changed our lives. For some of us the story is full of action and drama. For others of us, it may be quiet and with little fanfare, but it is personally our unique experience. I sometimes feel that my life's story is not worth sharing because it lacks intense highs and lows, heightened conflicts, and miraculous resolutions.

But "every individual has a life distinct from all others, and an experience differing essentially from theirs. God desires that our praise shall ascend to Him, marked by our own individuality. It is for our own benefit to keep every gift of God fresh in our memory. Thus faith is strengthened to claim and to receive more and more. There is greater encouragement for us in the least blessing we ourselves receive from God than in all the accounts we can read of the faith and experience of others."[xi]

Jesus calls us out because He uses our testimonies to encourage and embolden others to try God for themselves. As the praise text says: *O* [you] *taste the Lord and see that the Lord is good* (Psalm 34:8).

People can debate theological points, but when we share what God has done for us, it is real and personal. Others' decisions to accept or reject our testimonies is their gain or loss.

DAY 60

BIBLE TEXT: Luke 8:48 *And he said unto her, Daughter, be of good comfort: go in peace.*

BIBLE REFERENCES: Matthew 9; Mark 5; Luke 8

---

*B*e *of good comfort. Go in peace.* What a benediction and affirmation Jesus gave the woman with an issue of blood. She received that day more than the healing of her illness. She heard Jesus saying that everything in her life's space was now all right, and her journey would be protected. Never again was she to allow the devil to intimidate her. His roar was something she could safely ignore. Jesus gave her peace that passes all understanding (Philippians 4:7) for the future and that is good comfort!

It seems to be an accepted fact that there is a relationship between emotional and physical health, based upon repeated studies showing that faith and courage are in themselves very important components of healing prescriptions.

We need Jesus' affirmation of good comfort, especially when our physical, emotional, and spiritual worlds fall apart. However, only those who have been at Jesus' feet can have that peace because Jesus calls us "daughters" and bids us go in peace *after* we have been at His feet—after we have spent time with Him. And only those who have been at Jesus' feet will hear, *Well done thy good and faithful servant . . . enter thou into the joy of thy Lord* (Matthew

25:23). Sometimes we have the luxury of extended quiet moments with Him. Sometimes we don't. Many times, it is no more than a cry as we summon the last of our fading energies to reach out in faith for the hem of His garment.

When I was younger, I got tired of the old folks saying, "Pray about it." But as I add on years, I want my first response to every-thing, including finding a parking space, to be, "Pray about it."

We must fight against the temptation to live lives of perpetual activity to the exclusion of time needed for prayer, study, and spiri-tual meditation. "We are not to 'go' until we are endued. God can do more through us in five minutes when we are endued than we can do in a week alone. Though true love begins at the cross, all true service begins at our personal Pentecost."[xii]

Our personal moments with Jesus enable us to have serial vic-tories, miraculous healings, and fresh experiences to share with and encourage others.

When God shows up and shows out in all His glory, grace, and mercy to bring peace to our lives, He expects us to tell somebody! Let's not hide our blessings under a bushel! Let's constantly renew His affirmation of good comfort and peace.

MERAB (David's Denied Wife)

DAY 61

BIBLE TEXT: 1 Samuel 18:19 *But it came to pass at the time when Merab Saul's daughter should have been given to David, that she was given unto Adriel the Meholathite to wife.*

BIBLE REFERENCES: 1 Samuel 14, 17, 18

---

*M*erab's experience confirms that royal blood did not protect Old Testament women from their men folk's schemes and trickery. Merab was Saul's oldest daughter (1 Samuel 14), whom he promised to the warrior who slew Goliath (1 Samuel 17). David slew Goliath, but just as Laban double-crossed Jacob by giving him Leah instead of Rachel (Genesis 29), so King Saul tricked David by denying him Merab.

The Bible records that after David slew Goliath, he went to the palace and began his musical ministry for King Saul (1 Samuel 18). No doubt, wedding plans were needed so a delay would have been reasonable. Besides, having David close by allowed the King to become better acquainted with his future son-in-law.

However, something else was happening. David had already earned the right to marry Merab, so why did King Saul require him to continue fighting, *only be thou valiant for me, and fight the*

Lord's battles. As a side note, the verse continued, *For Saul said, Let not mine hand be upon him, but let the hand of the Philistines be upon him* (1 Samuel 18:17). The King expected David to die in battle. He did not and at the time when the marriage should have occurred, Merab was married to Adriel. King Saul's actions manifested his budding envy and jealousy of David.

In my junior year of college, I determined to earn a 4.0 grade point average. The professors were clear about their grading policies and work expectations. In a journalism class, I diligently applied myself, keeping an accurate account of the points awarded for each assignment. Based upon the class syllabus, I had earned an "A" grade. The professor did not give me an "A" and when I asked why, he simply replied that he did not think I deserved an "A."

I remember crying in the academic dean's office about being cheated out of a hard earned grade. It was all in vain. Even to this day, I recall the utter disappointment and despair I felt that a professor could so nonchalantly disregard his own syllabus, deny me my grade, and there was nothing I could do about it.

The next quarter, I determined to make a "F." I selected French as the class in which I would do absolutely nothing. I do not remember doing much more than attending classes, and by my records I earned at least a "D," but a strange thing happened. On my report card was a "C." What a lesson in merit and grace! When I had earned an "A," I got a "B"; when I had earned a "D," I received a "C."

I graduated, and the French professor will never know how much he influenced my life. Life is not fair, but grace happens. Share the good news.

MICHAL (David's Wife #1)

DAY 62

BIBLE TEXT: 1 Samuel 18:20 *And Michal Saul's daughter loved David: and they told Saul, and the thing pleased him.*

BIBLE REFERENCES: 1 Samuel 14, 18, 19, 25; 2 Samuel 3, 6, 21; 1 Chronicles 15

---

*M*ichal was Merab's younger sister, King Saul's second daughter (1 Samuel 14). Whatever Merab felt about her father's refusal to give her to David, Michal was delighted! She loved David. It showed; everyone else knew it, so they told her father. And that pleased him because Michal's love for David became the basis of her father's plotting. King Saul spread the rumor, via his servants, that he was pleased with David and looked forward to David becoming his son-in-law. 1 Samuel 18 tells the saga.

David, of course, was a poor shepherd and had no dowry to give for Michal's hand in marriage. King Saul sent word to David that 100 "foreskins of the Philistines" was an adequate dowry. Hopefully, King Saul thought, this time David would be killed in battle. Instead, David brought back 200 foreskins. Since the King could not go back on his widely publicized deal, David married Michal.

King Saul's under-the-table schemes to rid himself of David had failed. King *Saul saw and knew that the Lord was with David, and that Michal Saul's daughter loved him* (1 Samuel 18:28). But his hostility toward and hatred, envy, and jealousy of David continued to fester and grow. It was only a matter of time before King Saul would again seek David's life.

While the old advertising technique of "bait and switch" is not exactly on point, King Saul's actions are similar. "Bait and switch" advertising occurs when customers are offered a highly desirable product or service at an advertised "deal of a lifetime" price, but the store really has no intention of selling that item. The advertisement is simply to get the customers into the store where they are offered another version of the product—at a higher price! Laws have been enacted to prohibit "bait and switch" sales techniques. Most stores now disclose how many of an item they have in stock or clearly advertise that they have limited quantities of the hot ticket item.

The devil is the all time master of "bait and switch" advertising.

DAY 63

BIBLE TEXT: 1 Samuel 19:11 *Saul also sent messengers unto David's house, to watch him, and to slay him in the morning: and Michal David's wife told him, saying, If thou save not thy life to night, tomorrow thou shalt be slain.*

BIBLE REFERENCES: 1 Samuel 14, 18, 19, 25; 2 Samuel 3, 6, 21; 1 Chronicles 15

---

*M*ichal's father, King Saul, was given to fits of rage and outbursts of uncontrolled anger, which put her husband in great danger. Before her father had refused to allow Merab to marry David, he had thrown his javelin at David. 1 Samuel 19 reports another episode of King Saul throwing the javelin at David. Saul's envy and hatred of David had become so intense that Saul was determined to kill him.

David's escape from Saul's second javelin throw resulted in Saul's open plan to kill his daughter's husband. Saul sent messengers to David's house with instructions to kill him in the morning. How Michal knew that *If* [David] *save not thy life to night, tomorrow thou shalt be slain,* we are not told. Maybe she just put two-and-two together. Or maybe her brother, Jonathan, got word to her. Possibly the same servants, who had helped Saul spread the rumor about Saul being delighted with David, double-crossed the double-crossing, lying King who had murder on his mind.

Michal devised a plan to save her husband's life. Like Rahab, she was willing to take a big risk and deceive the King, rather than permit any harm to come to God's anointed. *So Michal let David down through a window: and he went, and fled, and escaped* (1 Samuel 19:12).

My father taught his eight children many lessons through illustrations and short stories. It is also my preferred way of making and sharing a point. Stories or parables, as Jesus demonstrated, remain with the hearers long after the theory and arguments are forgotten. To teach us the importance of inviting the Holy Spirit to guide us each day, my father shared a story about beginning our day of activity and suddenly remembering that we forgot an item at home and turning around to get it. He said that the devil had prepared holes for our feet to stumble into, and we would visualize our uplifted legs as we were about to place them down, but then in mid-air changing our minds as we heard a "little quiet voice" saying to change directions. We were, he stressed, to immediately obey the "little quiet voice."

Even today, when I am delayed in traffic or otherwise running late in spite of preparation to be on time, I remember my father teaching that the angels are protecting us from dangers ahead. The delay is for our own good and safety. *The angel of the Lord encampeth round about them that fear him, and delivereth them* (Psalm 34:7).

But the reverse side of this thinking is that whatever happens is within God's will, because He ordained that the "incident" should occur for His divine reason and purpose. That is not always so easy to see, sense, feel, or appreciate. Yet, the underlying fundamental principle of the Bible and the conflict between good and evil, God and Satan, can be summed up in Romans 8:28: *And we know that all things work together for good to them that love God, to them who are the called according to his purpose.*

Try applying these texts to your next "incident." God may be allowing you to escape through a window . . .

DAY 64

BIBLE TEXT: 1 Samuel 19:17 *And Michal answered Saul, He said unto me, Let me go; why should I kill thee?*

BIBLE REFERENCES: 1 Samuel 14, 18, 19, 25; 2 Samuel 3, 6, 21; 1 Chronicles 15

---

1 Samuel 19 tells the rest of the story. Once David fled, Michal *took an image, and laid it in the bed, and put a pillow of goats' hair for his bolster, and covered it with a cloth.* In the morning when *Saul sent messengers to take David, she said, 'He is sick.' And Saul sent the messengers again to see David, saying, bring him up to me in the bed, that I may slay him.*

When the messengers returned the second time, they looked, pulled back the covers, and discovered the image. Michal's assessment of King Saul's intentions was correct. He wanted David even if it required bringing him in his bed!

Trickery is a common thread running throughout human interactions. It is important to specify that trickery is only within evil spheres of interactions, since *God is not a man, that he should lie; neither the son of man, that he should repent: hath he said, and shall he not do it? or spoken, and shall he not make it good?* (Numbers 23:19).

Little white lies are a category of trickery. Our society permits a little white lie when telling the truth will "hurt" someone's feelings or when it serves a higher goal. The problem is that lies are always bad because we do not know what fruit the lies will yield. When Michal's father questioned her, he wanted to know, *Why hast thou deceived me so, and sent away mine enemy, that he is escaped?* (1 Samuel 19:17). Michal had learned well from her father's treacherous ways.

She lied about David's intentions, reporting that her life was in danger if she did not help him escape from Saul. However good her motives were, the Bible implies that Michal's lie finally gave her father Saul the "legitimate" reason to pursue and kill David; he had threatened Michal's life.

Consider the summarized "White Lie Cake"[xiii] story:

New to the church and community of friends, Alice Grayson wanted to participate in the Baptist Church Ladies' Group in Tuscaloosa, Alabama. On the morning of the Group's bake sale, Alice Grayson remembered that she was to bake a cake. Rummaging through cabinets, she found an angel food cake mix and quickly made the cake, but when she took the cake from the oven, the center had dropped flat and the cake was horribly disfigured. She did not have time to bake another cake. Being inventive, she found in the bathroom a roll of toilet paper to build up the center of the cake, which she plunked into the cake and covered it with icing. Not only did the finished product look beautiful, it looked perfect.

Before leaving the house to deliver the cake to the church, Alice woke her daughter Amanda giving her specific instructions to be at the bake sale the moment it opened at 9:30 a.m. to buy the cake and bring it home. When Amanda arrived at the sale, she found the attractive, perfect cake had already been sold. She grabbed her cell phone and called her mom.

Alice was horrified. All night, Alice lay awake in bed thinking about people pointing fingers at her and talking about her behind her back.

The next day, she prepared to attend a fancy luncheon/bridal shower at the home of a fellow church member who more than once had looked down her nose at Alice because she was a single parent and not from the founding families of Tuscaloosa.

The meal was elegant; the company was definitely upper-crust old-South. To Alice's horror, the cake was presented for dessert!

She started out of her chair to tell the hostess all about it, but before she could get to her feet, the mayor's wife said, "What a beautiful cake!" Alice, still stunned, sat back in her chair when she heard the hostess (who was a prominent church member) say, "Thank you, I baked it myself."

Alice smiled and thought to herself, "God is good."

DAY 65

BIBLE TEXT: 2 Samuel 3:14 *And David sent messengers to Ishbosheth Saul's son, saying, Deliver me my wife Michal, which I espoused to me for an hundred foreskins of the Philistines.*

BIBLE REFERENCES: 1 Samuel 14, 18, 19, 25; 2 Samuel 3, 6, 21; 1 Chronicles 15

---

*I*n 1 Samuel 25, the Bible reports that Saul gave Michal to Phalli, probably because he interpreted David's "threat" to kill Michal as ending the marriage, as well as David's flight to the prophet Samuel as abandonment. Also, David married Abigail, Nabal's wife.

Michal's time with her second husband spanned the years that David ran from her father. After Saul's death, his youngest surviving son was made king of Israel, supported by his uncle, Abner (2 Samuel 1 and 2). When a rift occurred between them, Abner offered Israel to David and David in turn demanded the return of Michal (2 Samuel 3). When the demand for Michal's return was made to the king, who was Michal's half-brother, he acquiesced to David's claim. Michal was returned to David, and her husband Phalli *went with her along weeping behind her* (2 Samuel 3:16), until Abner commanded him to return home.

What a mess! Even though Michal loved David, she had been with Phalli for twenty years or more. That he followed behind her weeping implies that their arranged marriage had grown into love and mutual respect. Did David really think that they could just pick up where they were the night she saved his life? What about Michal's feelings and thoughts about leaving her home and her life with Phalli?

As a judge, I preside over adoptions. Each one is a high point of my day. Some couples adopt infants who are of different nationalities, races, and ethnic backgrounds. Some families are literally a little "United Nations." Step-parent adoptions are especially satisfying because then all of the family members have the same last name. Grandparent adoptions are common. Occasionally, there are adults who are adopted by another adult as a part of an overall estate planning scheme.

Sometimes the stories behind the adoptions are heart breaking, such as the grandparents who adopted their grandsons because their father killed their mother; or often, due to drug addictions, the natural parents are unable or unwilling to rear the child. Rarely, second adoptions are necessary because either the first adopting parent rejects the child or the first adopting parent is dying.

When I conduct adoption court and the adoption includes children old enough to understand, I always explain to them how special they are because adoption means being intentionally and specially chosen by the parents. Of all the children in the world, their new parents had selected them to be their children. Natural born children are not handpicked by their parents, so being adopted makes them particularly loved and special.

Nevertheless, many adopted children want to know about their roots, and if they are old enough to remember their natural parents, there is always a special place in their hearts for them. As soon as they are able to research their early childhood, many adopted children investigate and trace their biological family tree.

And many parents never forget the child given up for adoption.

DAY 66

BIBLE TEXT: 1 Chronicles 15:29 *And it came to pass, as the ark of the covenant of the Lord came to the city of David, that Michal, the daughter of Saul looking out at a window saw king David dancing and playing: and she despised him in her heart.*

BIBLE REFERENCES: 1 Samuel 14, 18, 19, 25; 2 Samuel 3, 6, 21; 1 Chronicles 15

---

*T*he above text from 1 Chronicles 15 reports only the beginning of the story about Michal's response to David's exultance upon the return of the Ark to Jerusalem. The rest of the story is provided in 2 Samuel 6. Why Michal would despise David is left to our imagination. Maybe she was bitter about being forced to leave Phalli and their family; or she resented being one of David's growing number of wives; or her personality did not value David's personality; or quite simply, she no longer loved David.

But whatever the reason, Michal was sorely displeased with David's display of dancing, playing of his instrument, and his worshipping joyously because the Ark had been safely brought to Jerusalem. And she told him so!

Michal *came out to meet David, and said, How glorious was the king of Israel to day, who uncovered himself to day in the eyes of the handmaids of his servants, as one of the vain fellows shamelessly uncovereth himself!* What a strong rebuke before giving David an opportunity to explain his actions. David was more than just her husband; he was God's handpicked king of Israel and Judah. Maybe God saw that Michal's despising of David's worship was like the people's demand for a king; it had not been a rejection of Samuel, the prophet, but a rejection of God's leadership (1 Samuel 8).

God does not force people to choose Him; consider Deuteronomy 30. My experience in drug court confirms that until addicts want to change, all the programs designed to help are underused resources. As hard as it may sound, letting addicts hit rock bottom is the first step of recovery; they must decide they do not want to be there. What anyone thinks or feels or how they react to the addicts' choices is irrelevant; it really is all about the addicts' choices.

Likewise, one's style of praise is personal. This is a concept many people find hard to grasp, appreciate, and respect. God fashioned each of us uniquely and particularly, so as my Grandfather said, "We each have a different nose." Is it a shock to our minds to think for one moment that our attempt to define for others their style of praise is based upon an underlying motivation to control others to be like us? We are quiet, so we want everyone in our space to be quiet. We are energetic, so we want everyone in our space to be energetic. We can compose hundreds of thoughts along this analysis. We are most comfortable with what we know and with what we are familiar.

The Ten Commandments establish ground zero of man's behavior (Exodus 20). Jesus summed them up when He said, *Thou shalt love the Lord thy God with all thy heart, and with all thy soul, and with all thy mind. This is the first and great commandment. And the second is like unto it, Thou shalt love thy neighbour as thyself. On these two commandments hang all the law and the prophets* (Matthew 22:37-40). How we manifest love for our neighbor is the challenge.

So why do we want to force others to be like us?

DAY 67

BIBLE TEXT: 2 Samuel 6:21 *And David said unto Michal, It was before the Lord, which chose me before thy father, and before all his house, to appoint me ruler over the people of the Lord, over Israel: therefore will I play before the Lord.*

BIBLE REFERENCES: 1 Samuel 14, 18, 19, 25; 2 Samuel 3, 6, 21; 1 Chronicles 15

*D*avid pointed out to Michal that the people understood and appreciated his unrestrained acts of worship and praise; he absolutely rejected Michal's reprimand. Because of God's blessings upon him, he reminded her, he would praise God even more gloriously. Nothing Michal did or said would cause David to forget God's hand of protection and gifts of success. His praise was as he wrote in Psalm 150:

Praise ye the Lord. Praise God in his sanctuary: praise him in the firmament of his power.

Praise him for his mighty acts: praise him according to his excellent greatness.

Praise him with the sound of the trumpet: praise him with the psaltery and harp.

Praise him with the timbrel and dance: praise him with stringed instruments and organs.

Praise him upon the loud cymbals: praise him upon the high sounding cymbals.

Let everything that hath breath praise the Lord, Praise ye the Lord.

I had many rich experiences visiting churches during my two judicial election campaigns. In those services, I came to realize that people experience God in a myriad of ways. The sincerity of their love, respect, commitment, and devotion was apparent. Visiting these churches was excellent preparation for my later mission trips into other countries and cultures.

Heaven is filled with worship and praise. John the Revelator describes in Revelation 4 and 5 how the four living creatures are joined by the 24 elders; then they are joined by the heavenly choir; then these three groups are joined by every creature in the entire universe in praise to God the Father and to Jesus the Lamb of God.

Maybe in Heaven we will realize that our expression of praise on earth should have had a little more volume. . . .

DAY 68

BIBLE TEXT: 2 Samuel 6:23 *Therefore Michal the daughter of Saul had no child unto the day of her death.*

BIBLE REFERENCES: 1 Samuel 14, 18, 19, 25; 2 Samuel 3, 6, 21; 1 Chronicles 15

---

*G*od's response to Michal's rebuke of David's praise and worship was immediate, direct, and significant. At first blush, this seems like a very harsh and punitive sanction for either or both of her transgressions, i.e., speaking what she thought or devaluing another's worship. God closed her womb; she bore none of David's children. How interesting that God's rebuke was of the same ilk as her complaint.

Michal chided David, saying, *How glorious was the king of Israel to day, who uncovered himself to day in the eyes of the handmaids of his servants, as one of the vain fellows shamelessly uncovereth himself!* She saw David's actions as unworthy of a king and as common, uncouth behavior. She was embarrassed and humiliated.

God's chastisement went like an arrow to the core of Michal's analysis. He punished her lack of gratitude and appreciation by depriving her of what gave her status, worth, and value. She would forever be embarrassed, humiliated, whispered about, and pointed out as an example of the consequences when one is more concerned about pretending to be rather than being.

Sometimes when making a judicial decision, I pause for a moment to think about the public's probable reaction. Will I make the news or front page headlines? But my oath requires me to follow the "rule of law."

In junior high school, I remember learning Edgar Guest's poem, "Myself." For more than forty years, these particular lines have remained with me and influenced my decisions: "I don't want to keep on a closet shelf/ A lot of secrets about myself/ And fool myself, as I come and go, / Into thinking that nobody else will know . . . " These lines helped me to decide that I would not be blackmailed, intimidated, or embarrassed into making any unwise decisions.

It is still a poem worthy of memory and reflection.

Myself

I have to live with myself, and so
I want to be fit for myself to know, I want
to be able, as the days go by, Always to
look myself straight in the eye; I don't
want to stand, with the setting sun,
And hate myself for the things I have done.
I don't want to keep on a closet shelf
A lot of secrets about myself, And
fool myself, as I come and go,
Into thinking that nobody else will know
The kind of man I really am;

I don't want to dress up myself in sham.

I want to go out with my head erect,

I want to deserve all men's respect;

But here in the struggle for fame and pelf

I want to be able to like myself.

I don't want to look at myself and know

That I'm bluster and bluff and empty show.

I can never hide myself from me;

I see what others may never see;

I know what others may never know,

I never can fool myself, and so,

Whatever happens, I want to be

Self-respecting and conscience free.

DAY 69

BIBLE TEXT: 2 Samuel 21:8 *But the king took the two sons of Rizpah the daughter of Aiah, whom she bare unto Saul, Armoni and Mephibosheth; and the five sons of Michal the daughter of Saul, whom she brought up for Adriel the son of Barzillai the Meholathite.*
BIBLE REFERENCES: 1 Samuel 14, 18, 19, 25; 2 Samuel 3, 6, 21; 1 Chronicles 15

---

*M*ichal was barren because she rebuked David's high praise to God. Consequently, there must be an explanation for the Bible's reference to her five sons who were hanged beside two of Saul's sons because of Saul's slaughter of the Gibeonites. Was she barren after being reunited with David? Did she have sons by Phalli?

Since the text says *she brought up for Adriel*, most likely "the sons" were nephews. Adriel was married to Merab, Saul's oldest daughter, the one David was supposed to marry as a reward for slaying Goliath (1 Samuel 18). Maybe Merab died and her sons were reared by Aunt Michal. However Michal became responsible for the boys, it was of little consequence to David, who complied with the Gibeonites' request in full settlement for Saul's murderous actions.

David may have been willing to comply with the Gibeonites' request because he was conveniently settling his own scores for what he may have perceived as Saul's daughters' parts in Saul's plots against him. On another level, God ensured that none of David's seed would ever mingle with Saul's, since David had no children by either of Saul's daughters. God terminated King Saul's bloodline from kingship because of Saul's sins of rebellion and stubbornness (1 Samuel 15:23).

The Bible presents many challenges in understanding genealogy. Usually, only necessary biographical details related to the major point the author wanted to convey are provided. Maybe their oral history supplied the missing information.

For my family's 2006 reunion, I sought to trace our heritage. I learned that tracing family history in African American families before 1870 is very difficult and in many cases impossible. Prior to that time, slaves were counted in mass and by category. Their names and biographical information were never recorded or noted, so, summarily, it is almost as if they never existed. Families attempting to trace their lineage before and during slavery have to comb for information in public documents, such as census reports, and in private documents, such as wills.

Because the 1890 census was destroyed by fire, the gap in data made identifying family members more challenging since a major and important marker in naming family members was lost. Thus, grandchildren being reared by grandparents may have been counted as sons or daughters.

While we are not sure about Michal's sons, and families today are unable to completely trace their genealogies, we are sure that the ancestors existed. We just do not know where to correctly place them on the genealogy charts.

AHINOAM (David's Wife #2)

DAY 70

BIBLE TEXT: 1 Samuel 25:43 *David also took Ahinoam of Jezreel.*

BIBLE REFERENCES: 1 Samuel 25, 27, 30; 2 Samuel 2, 3; 1 Chronicles 3

---

*A*hinoam of Jezreel was David's wife. She is not to be confused with King Saul's wife of the same name, daughter of Ahimaaz (1 Samuel 14:50). In its normal recording of events and biographies, again the Bible cuts short any significant information about David's most likely second wife. She may have become his wife after Abigail, but since she is usually named before Abigail, for our purposes, she is considered as David's second wife.

In Bible days, at least two places were known as Jezreel. Ahinoam most likely was from Jezreel of Judah, a town southeast of Hebron (Joshua 15:56). The other Jezreel identified in 1 Kings 21 was associated with King Ahab who wanted the vineyard owned by "Naboth the Jezreelite." Ahab's wife, Jezebel, orchestrated Naboth's death so that Ahab could have the vineyard.

Just because so little is shared about Ahinoam, a faulty conclusion could be reached that she is insignificant in the overall life of David. However, the Bible disclosed that she was the mother of David's first-born son, Amnon, who raped and then despised Tamar, his half-sister and Absalom's sister (2 Samuel 13). The consequences of Ahinoam's son's actions eventually led to a civil war between David and Absalom (2 Samuel 15). We do not know whether Ahinoam lived to see the results of her son's choices, but surely she would have advised him against such a selfish sin and inconsiderate act.

For many parents, especially mothers, it is very hard to separate themselves from their children. Whatever their children do, they see it as a reflection upon themselves, since they always see the children as extensions of themselves, rather than accepting the reality that at an appropriate age children should be treated as free and independent people. It is as if the umbilical cord is never completely cut. This lack of independence is not emotionally or psychologically healthy. God allows us to make our decisions and to take the consequences of them. Our choices are a reflection upon us. God created Lucifer; Satan made himself (Ezekiel 28:15).

In my courtroom, a mother stood with her son who was on probation in another county. Many people consider probation as a delayed jail sentence because any new law violation committed anywhere allows the judge to impose the crime's maximum penalty. Usually, the entry of a plea to the new charge is considered as an admission of violation of probation.

The mother opined that because she did not believe his probation would be violated, her son would accept the plea offer for the new crime. As the judge, my conversation was directed to her son, the defendant. He was entitled to have an attorney appointed to assist him, but his mother zealously pushed him to waive this right and to enter a no contest plea to the new charge. Finally, I said to them, "Your mother cannot go to jail for you!"

I remember the case because too often people making decisions for other people do not have to suffer the consequences of the decisions. We are held responsible for our choices, even if "the devil made us do it."

DAY 71

BIBLE TEXT: 1 Samuel 27:3 *And David dwelt with Achish at Gath, he and his men, every man with his household, even David with his two wives, Ahinoam the Jezreelitess, . . .*

BIBLE REFERENCES: 1 Samuel 25, 27, 30; 2 Samuel 2, 3; 1 Chronicles 3

---

*A*hinoam went with David to Gath, in the land of the Philistines, when David sought refuge from King Saul's unrelenting hostility. 1 Samuel 25:7 states that David asked the king of Gath for *a place in some town in the country, that* [he] *may dwell there*. He was given the town of Ziklag.

While living in Philistine, David conducted numerous raids against other peoples living in Philistine territory, but he reported his conquests as if he had ventured into Judah. It was important that the son of the king of Gath believe that David was looting David's own people. This ruse continued for over a year. Surely, there was much discussion in Ziklag about David's actions, especially since David did not leave anyone alive to report anything differently from the official version of events. David's ruse was successful because the king's son came to completely trust David, thinking that he had *made his people Israel utterly to abhor him* (1 Samuel 27:12).

Ahinoam's son, Amnon, was born later (2 Samuel 3), but it is reasonable that he learned about this period of time when David's deceptions demonstrated a lack of faith and trust in God. It is said that children's characters are formed by the time they reach three years of age. While too young to articulate and interpret all of the events occurring around them, children's minds, nonetheless, are videotaping an accurate version of the events seen and words spoken.

Just like there are parents who do not allow their children the freedom and permission to develop into free independent adults, there are parents who do not take responsibility to role model appropriate behavior for their children. The parents are best described as hands-off or "laissez faire," whatever happens, happens. Children need parents to label and explain, model and practice appropriate behavior and thought processes. What is so embarrassing and hurtful to parents in the courtroom are those children whose behavior and choices clearly reject the parents' efforts to set a good example.

Parents probably cannot be too careful about their words and actions because children seem to see and hear everything! Their minds are being imprinted with decision-making processes based upon what adults are doing and saying. Preachers like to point out to parents that if after church dinner conversation is "serving up the pastor," then parents should not be surprised if their children have little respect for pastors and are disillusioned about the role of organized religion in their lives. "Bad habits are caught; good habits are taught," so the old adage says.

What are we allowing our children to catch?

DAY 72

BIBLE TEXT: 1 Samuel 30:5 *And David's two wives were taken captives, Ahinoam the Jezreelitess, . . .*

BIBLE REFERENCES: 1 Samuel 25, 27, 30; 2 Samuel 2, 3; 1 Chronicles 3

---

1 Samuel 29 records that war again broke out between the Philistines and King Saul, and God miraculously delivered David, who was living amongst the Philistines, from fighting against Israel. However, during the three days it took for David to go and return to Ziklag, the Amalekites invaded and burned Ziklag. The Amalekites had been raided by David during his deceptions to the Philistines about which people David raided.

The Amalekites were descendants of Esau, Jacob's twin brother. It was in battle against them that the children of Jacob (Israel) prevailed as long as Moses' hand was uplifted (Exodus 17). We remember this event because Moses called the altar he erected on that hill, *Jehovah Nissi*, "Jehovah my banner." King Saul's failure to destroy the Amalekites caused God to reject Saul as king of Israel (1 Samuel 15), and the centuries old hatred between the cousins came to a head when Haman attempted to murder all the Jews in the book of Esther.

Ahinoam was taken captive, along with all the other women and children. Unbeknown to their men, God miraculously did not allow the Amalekites to kill anyone. When the warriors returned home to their burned down city, they wept uncontrollably *until they had no more power to weep*. They wanted to stone David, *but David encouraged himself in the Lord his God* (1 Samuel 30: 6).

Did Ahinoam do the same or was all her hope gone and faith broken? The Amalekites had possibly three days' head start into the wilderness, and based upon all the undisputed evidence, the Amalekites would use her as a slave or sell her. David probably thought she was dead, sold, or gone without a trace. The chances of her being rescued were slim to none.

I notice that I "misplace" things more often these days, and I am greatly annoyed by the amount of time it takes me to find the items. Looking for them can become an all-consuming task, causing me to lose focus on other tasks, even sometimes making me irritated with God because He just does not show me where the item is patiently waiting for me to find it! These experiences are becoming a crisis of faith!

Can I discipline my mind to settle down, accept the frustration of not being able to find the item at this moment, and move on to other things? Or am I so focused on finding it that I cannot think straight?

On my good days, I remember Romans 8:28. On my bad days, it just takes me longer to remember Romans 8:28!

DAY 73

BIBLE TEXT: 2 Samuel 2:2 *So David went up thither, and his two wives also, Ahinoam the Jezreelitess, . . .*

BIBLE REFERENCES: 1 Samuel 25, 27, 30; 2 Samuel 2, 3; 1 Chronicles 3

When David returned safely to Ziklag with his wives and their possessions, as well as with all of his men's wives and their possessions, he learned that King Saul had died in battle. Ahinoam most likely joined David and his men as they grieved the death of King Saul. David summarily killed the Amalekite who brought news of King Saul's death, implying that he had killed "God's anointed" (2 Samuel 1).

David then inquired of the Lord if he should leave Ziklag and return to Judah. He was told to go to Hebron, the area of Ahinoam's home. Surely, she was happy to be home again and to be the wife of the next king of Israel! She had done well for herself.

Ahinoam's son, Amnon, was born in Hebron (1 Chronicles 3). As Ahinoam trained him as the honored first-born son, Amnon also learned of his father's conquests and deeds. He was, after all, the son of David, the mighty warrior of Judah, slayer of giants and doer of many great and wonderful deeds. Each child inherits tendencies towards good and evil from every preceding generation, and those tendencies combine together to create a new person uniquely different from all the others before *or after*.

Amnon inherited his father's tendency toward deceit, quick thinking, scheming, and premeditated sin. Amnon raped his half-sister, Tamar, which set in motion revenge by her brother, Absalom (2 Samuel 13). And that set in motion Absalom's rebellion against David. But these events were fulfilling prophecies because of David's premeditated sin involving another man's wife, Bathsheba.

The Bible teaches that the choices parents make, good or bad, continue from one generation to another. Consider the instructions provided in the second commandment, *For I the Lord thy God am a jealous God, visiting the iniquity of the fathers upon the children unto the third and fourth generation of them that hate me; And shewing mercy unto thousands of them that love me, and keep my command-ments* (Exodus 20:5-6).

But also consider, the Bible teaches that each person is respon-sible for his or her own choices. Jesus said in Matthew 12:36, *But I say unto you, That every idle word that men shall speak, they shall give account thereof in the day of judgment*.

It is in this tension that parents are to find balance for coping with their children's decisions. Parents can strive to do their very best and children will still make unwise decisions. It is the nature of life. It is the consequence of our God-given freedom of choice. It is the nature of sin. It is the reproduction on earth of the conflict in heaven.

While an attorney, I once went to court with a dear friend whose child was being sentenced for a crime. My plea to the judge, a personal friend, was for mercy, not so much for the wayward child but for the parents because of the impact the sentence would have on them. The child's sentence was not particularly changed by our requests for mercy. It was a strange experience to beg for mercy and receive little.

ABIGAIL (David's Wife #3)

DAY 74

BIBLE TEXT: 1 Samuel 25:3 *Now the name of the man was Nabal; and the name of his wife Abigail: and she was a woman of good understanding, and of a beautiful countenance: but the man was churlish and evil in his doings; and he was of the house of Caleb.*

BIBLE REFERENCES: 1 Samuel 25, 27, 30; 2 Samuel 2, 3; 1 Chronicles 3

---

*A*bigail, David's third wife, fostered different aspects of David's growth. By deceit, Michal saved David from her father's hatred. By kindness, Abigail saved David from himself. 1 Samuel 25 records their story.

Leaving behind his wife, Michal, David fled from King Saul to Ramah, where the prophet Samuel lived. David remained in Ramah until Samuel died. Then David fled into the wilderness, where he and his men protected Nabal's servants and large flocks from attacks by roving tribes. Nabal's name meant "fool" and he was a fool. (Did his mother name him "fool," or did Nabal become his name because he often acted like a fool?) While Nabal was a descendant of Caleb, he did not share Caleb's character. Caleb had agreed with Joshua that the children of Israel could conquer the Promised Land (Numbers

13 and 14).

When David learned that Nabal was shearing his sheep in Carmel, he sent ten young men to ask for food. This was a reasonable request.

Nabal's foolish response brought Abigail into David's life. She was beautiful and, unlike Nabal, she was *a woman of good understanding* (1 Samuel 25:3).

While opposites may attract, studies reveal that the most successful marriages are those in which the partners are actually more alike than different in the key areas of intelligence, trust, acceptance, and genuineness.[xiv] Chances are Nabal and Abigail's marriage was not a happy one. It seems they had very little in common.

When I practiced family law, it seemed to me that there was a direct correlation between the intensity of the love at the beginning of the marriage and the intensity of the fighting when the marriage was over. The more in love a spouse was at the time of marriage, the more hurt, disappointed, and bitter he or she would be at the time of dissolution of the marriage.

Another interesting observation was when a spouse knew the marriage was over. Some said they knew as they walked down the aisle, or on the honeymoon night. While it may have taken 20 years before the final divorce decree, the clients' question was, "How quickly can the judge end a dead relationship?"

However, I found the saddest cases were those in which one spouse knew early on that the marriage was doomed but the other spouse had no idea. The unsuspecting spouse would do anything to save the marriage, but the other spouse had long ago decided he or she simply wanted out. Good examples were cases when spouses stayed until the last child graduated from high school or college. The child's sheepskin was symbolic of the parents' pending divorce papers.

DAY 75

BIBLE TEXT: 1 Samuel 25:14 *But one of the young men told Abigail, Nabal's wife, saying, Behold, David sent messengers out of the wilderness to salute our master; and he railed on them.*

BIBLE REFERENCES: 1 Samuel 25, 27, 30; 2 Samuel 2, 3; 1 Chronicles 3

---

*I*n 1 Samuel 25, Nabal not only rebuked David, but also arrogantly refused to give David food and sustenance in recognition of David's protection of Nabal's men and flocks. Nabal neither appreciated nor recognized that David and his *men were very good unto us*. David's protection had been like *a wall unto us both by night and day, all the while we were with them keeping the sheep*. Nabal's herdsmen *were not hurt, neither missed anything . . . when we were in the fields*. Upon the ten young men's delivery of Nabal's reply, David promptly decided to rid the earth of such a rude, coarse, and unpleasant person.

Fortunately, one of Nabal's servants quickly and accurately assessed the perilous situation. Immediately he told Abigail that the entire settlement was in danger because of Nabal's ungrateful and stingy response. What a tribute to her character and influence that the young servant knew what to do, who to tell, and was not afraid to talk to Abigail. He knew that Abigail would appreciate knowing about Nabal's foolish actions. Most likely in prior situations, based upon other servants' reports, Abigail had run interference for Nabal. "Knowledge is a powerful thing," so the saying goes, but kindness is more powerful. Limited communication occurs when deliverers of the message defensively say, "Don't shoot the messenger!" Important and valuable information is never shared because of how hearers react.

My friend, Patrisha, tells the story of her sister's forced and unhappy move across country. Her nephew excitedly tried to tell his mother something which he thought was very important, but her sister, in a dejected state of mind, refused to hear anything her young son wanted to share. Although he was persistent, her angry attitude, sharp words, and mean tone shut him down. When they arrived in Tallahassee, all their belongings packed on top of the car were gone because the roof top storage bin was open. That was what the little boy had tried to tell his mother.

Far too often we find that our own attitude about the messenger clouds our ability to hear or appreciate the value of the message. Our disrespect for the status or position of the messenger causes us to think that there is nothing they can tell us. If we were visiting in an exclusive home and the house was on fire, would it really matter that the servant sounded the warning rather than the homeowner?

DAY 76

BIBLE TEXT: 1 Samuel 25:18 *Then Abigail made haste, and took two hundred loaves, and two bottles of wine, and five sheep ready dressed, and five measures of parched corn, and an hundred clusters of raisins, and two hundred cakes of figs, and laid them on asses.*

BIBLE REFERENCES: 1 Samuel 25, 27, 30; 2 Samuel 2, 3; 1 Chronicles 3

---

*T*he servant's message in 1 Samuel 25 also included this evaluation of Nabal: *Our master, . . . is such a son of Belial, that a man cannot speak to him.* Severe and serious danger to life and limb lurked just miles away. Sometimes it is wise to analyze and act simultaneously. Long reflective thought, hesitation, delayed action, or consultation with the head of the house are not always appropriate, and in this case were actually counter-productive. Abigail's response revealed that she was not only wise, but also a woman who took appropriate and expeditious action, thereby confirming the servant's excellent decision to promptly tell her what Nabal had done.

She immediately ordered her servants to take food supplies and go ahead of her to David. She ordered them not to say anything to her husband. She then rode on her donkey to meet David. *And when Abigail saw David, she hasted, and lighted off the ass, and fell before David on her face, and bowed herself to the ground, and fell at his feet, and said, Upon me, my lord, upon me let this iniquity be: and let thine handmaid, I pray thee, speak in thine audience, and hear the words of thine handmaid.*"

David must have been stunned by Abigail's poise, grace, humility, beauty, and ardor.

Confronting an enemy with a soft answer is disarming; the Bible says so! *A soft answer turneth away wrath: but grievous words stir up anger* (Proverbs 15:1). But it is hard to meet harsh words with kind words! There is another text we would prefer to apply, *Eye for eye, tooth for tooth, hand for hand, foot for foot* (Exodus 21:24). Yet, Jesus settled once and for all which text controls, Y*e have heard that it hath been said, An eye for an eye, and a tooth for a tooth: But I say unto you, That ye resist not evil: but whosoever shall smite thee on thy right cheek, turn to him the other also* (Matthew 5:38-39).

I was shopping in Lowe's store and I noticed the next customer intensely studying me. I thought the woman was trying to remember where she had seen me as I prepared to admit that I was a judge, or at least worked in the courthouse. Instead, she rebuked me for cutting off "all" my hair, pointing out that a woman's hair is her glory.[xv] Only the Holy Spirit gave me this retort: "Thank you for sharing." And I said it with a smile on my face, in my voice, and in my heart!

I thought I could see the wind gush out of her sails—no argument or scene. No opportunity to forcefully push her point or embarrass me by her experienced knowledge. I calmly walked out of the store, leaving her to grasp what had just happened.

DAY 77

BIBLE TEXT: 1 Samuel 25:27 *And now this blessing which thine handmaid hath brought unto my lord, let it even be given unto the young men that follow my lord.*

BIBLE REFERENCES: 1 Samuel 25, 27, 30; 2 Samuel 2, 3; 1 Chronicles 3

---

*T*he story continues in 1 Samuel 25. As Abigail fell at David's feet, she asked to be heard and explained that her husband, Nabal, was, as his name meant, a fool. Further, like Moses of old, Abigail interceded on Nabal's behalf, appealing to David's better nature to overlook Nabal's foolish response *because she had not seen or received David's ten men and wanted David to forgive her trespass of not graciously accepting his request for food.*

Abigail told David that as God's anointed he had fought many righteous battles for the Lord, but innocent people would die if he took revenge against Nabal into his own hands. She explained further, *And it shall come to pass, when the Lord shall have done to my lord according to all the good that he hath spoken concerning thee, and shall have appointed thee ruler over Israel; that this shall be no grief unto thee, nor offence of heart unto my lord, either that thou hast shed blood causeless, or that my lord hath avenged himself: but when the Lord shall have dealt well with my lord, then remember thine handmaid.*

The wisdom and insight of her words were not wasted. *David said to Abigail, Blessed be the Lord God of Israel, which sent thee this day to meet me.* Her quick thinking and gracious actions prevented Nabal's death by David's hands.

Once I was sharing with my good friend Teresa and her husband, Anthony, that it is so important to let God handle your enemies and the story of Moses and Korah in Numbers 16 came to mind. Korah and his supporters challenged Moses' authority, stating that the entire congregation was holy and Moses had lifted himself up above the rest of the people. God responded through Moses by telling the people to step away from Korah, his tent, and his possessions. Then the earth opened and swallowed everything and everyone who joined Korah's rebellion. The object lesson is to be sure that we are on God's side when God executes judgment, lest we are consumed by His judgment.

Maybe we have seen God execute "earth swallowing" judgments upon those who object to, suppress, or ignore His clear revelations. Financially, we can receive blessings as promised in Malachi 3:10-12, or suffer curses as recorded in Matthew 6:19, if our treasures are *where moth and rust corrupt and thieves break in to steal.*

God does not need our help to settle the score with our enemies because they are His enemies also. He knows the right strategy and He has the best plan because He has all of the information and facts to fashion the most appropriate resolutions.

DAY 78

BIBLE TEXT: 1 Samuel 25:36 *And Abigail came to Nabal; and, behold, he held a feast in his house, like the feast of a king; and Nabal's heart was merry within him, for he was very drunken: wherefore she told him nothing, less or more, until the morning light.*

BIBLE REFERENCES: 1 Samuel 25, 27, 30; 2 Samuel 2, 3; 1 Chronicles 3

---

*D*avid accepted Abigail's advice and food supplies. He saw the foolishness of his ways and repented of his purpose to ensure that neither Nabal nor anything that belonged to him would be left alive the next morning. Abigail had saved her own life by interceding for Nabal. David dismissed her, telling her to *Go up in peace to thine house; see, I have hearkened to thy voice.*

It was late when Abigail returned from her encounter with David. Nabal, who was completely unaware of the danger in which he had placed himself, his family, his servants, and his flocks, ended the successful sheep shearing season with a feast fit for a king. It had been a superb season for the birth, growth, and care of the sheep. Food was plenteous and wine flowed freely. Nabal's joyful celebration caused him to become drunk. Abigail again demonstrated great wisdom and restraint. She said nothing to him until the morning.

When the sober Nabal heard the rest of the story, the magnitude of the danger frightened him so severely that he suffered a stroke-like condition, because *his heart died within him, and he became as a stone*. Ten days later he died. David blessed the Lord for keeping him from evil; Nabal suffered the consequences of his own wickedness.

There are so many applications from this snapshot of Abigail's story: Timing is everything. God does settle the score for injustices done to His children. The outcomes of our choices are sure and predictable. Others contribute to our success and are entitled to be acknowledged. Intemperate living has consequences. Fear kills.

As a child attending evangelistic meetings, I heard stories about women and children who wanted to be baptized, but their husbands and fathers strenuously objected. I recall preachers sharing how dangerous it was to stand in another's way of accepting Christ, referring to Matthew 18:6-7, where Jesus said it would be better for that person to have a millstone hung around his neck and be drowned in the depth of the sea than to interfere with another's desire to be saved.

The story was told of a man who told his wife she would be baptized over his dead body. After being baptized, she returned home and found him dead. This story lingers with me today because it impressed upon me the seriousness of human interference with God's call for our repentance and our acceptance of His offer of eternal life.

To some degree, we still face interference from others when we accept the Good News. If there is one point that is most clear from

Abigail's experience, it is this: Jesus left heaven and came to earth to seek the lost. Thus, the value He places upon each soul is so great He will allow no one, no being, and no event to *separate us from the love of God, which is in Christ Jesus our Lord* (Romans 8:39).

DAY 79

BIBLE TEXT: 1 Chronicles 3:1 *Now these were the sons of David, which were born unto him in Hebron; the firstborn Amnon, of Ahinoam the Jezreelitess; the second Daniel, of Abigail the Carmelitess:*

BIBLE REFERENCES: 1 Samuel 25, 27, 30; 2 Samuel 2, 3; 1 Chronicles 3

1 Samuel 25 recorded the happy ending of the rest of the story! When David learned of Nabal's death, he sent his servants to get Abigail. She quickly accepted David's proposal to become his third wife and immediately left with her five damsels (1 Samuel 25:40-42). She walked away from whatever she had known as Nabal's wife into the unknown as David's wife. But she knew God had anointed David as Israel's next king, and, in faith, she joined her future to his.

What is quite interesting about the last of Abigail's story is that she had a son, Daniel, also known as Chileab (2 Samuel 3:3). And this is all we know about him. It is clear that he was not counted in the fourfold death sentence which resulted from David's adulterous relationship with Bathsheba (2 Samuel 11 and 12), but his contemporary brothers were affected by the sentence.

Why did David's second son cease to exist in Bible history? Did Daniel die? Was he sickly or otherwise unable to serve as king? Were there questions about his paternity? Why did Solomon, a much younger half-brother, become God's chosen heir to David's throne?

Maybe because of his mother's wisdom and insight, Daniel realized that he was not "king material" and was content to be David's son, without any desire for the throne or threat to God's will about who would inherit David's throne.

Studies have sought to identify characteristics of children based upon their birth order. A quick perusal of the Internet led me to an article[xvi] which acknowledges that there are many myths about children's IQ and personality due to birth order. In summary, first-borns, because of the unshared high quality attention from their parents, are destined to be responsible leaders and problem solvers, with higher IQs and better relationships with adults. Of course, they could also be quite susceptible to "guilt trips," since they "must" set the example for the younger siblings.

Middle children, on the other hand, are the negotiators and peacemakers since they have to bridge the communications gap between the older and younger siblings. Upon adulthood, they want to be as far removed from the family as possible to finally have the opportunity to develop into their own selves! They are no longer in the shadow of the first-born or competing for attention against the youngest.

Supposedly, last-born children are spoiled because by the time they arrive, parents do not have the energy to "fight the good fight!" The older children seem to be doing just fine, so why, the tired parents ask themselves, should they pay intense attention to every detail and concern. Of course, the older children are appalled by the parents' "laissez faire" attitude! Youngest children are perceived as possessing selfish and self-centered goals.

It will be so interesting to look at God's heavenly records and learn more about Daniel aka Chileab.

MAACAH (David's Wife #4)

DAY 80

BIBLE TEXT: 2 Samuel 3:3 [David's sons born in Hebron] . . . *the third, Absalom, the son of Maacah, the daughter of Talma, king of Geshur.*

BIBLE REFERENCES: 2 Samuel 3; 1 Chronicles 3

---

*M*aacah was of royal blood and most likely taken as a sign of David's victory over her father. Since she is not mentioned until after Michal, Ahinoam, and Abigail, she can be considered David's fourth wife. Like Ahinoam, Maacah is known for her son, Absalom, and his sister, Tamar.

Maacah's father was the ruler of a territory in northern Syria, which had been allotted to the half-tribe of Manasseh. Her people, the inhabitants of Geshur, were never fully expelled from the land.[xvii] Whether she was a trophy of war or a political bride is not clear. However, it is quite possible that Maacah taught Absalom that because he was the son and grandson of kings, he was predestined to be king over *both* Israel and Geshur. Thus, it is easier to understand why Absalom willingly rebelled against his father and brought civil war to the nation.

If Maacah was a trophy of war, Absalom may have been settling the score for his wronged mother. He had already demonstrated that he would settle injustices done to his family by taking matters into his own hands—he killed Amnon for raping his sister Tamar (2 Samuel 13). Afterwards, he fled to Geshur, his mother's home, and stayed there three years.

Absalom's pagan heritage caused him not to respect God's selection of David's successor. In Absalom's mind, his birth order made him next in line for David's throne, since Amnon was dead and Daniel was not a threat.

Only in heaven will we learn whether Maacah encouraged her son's choices which eventually resulted in his death (2 Kings 18). Sometimes parents are blamed for the choices their children make. We seem to treat as common knowledge that parental influence overrides individual freedom of choice, but that is not necessarily so. There have been far too many parents in my courtroom, standing alongside their children, and it is obvious that the children were not reared to disrespect themselves, their families, or the law.

Ted Bundy, a serial killer, gave his final interview to Dr. James Dobson of Focus on the Family. I distinctly remember reading about the interview back in 1989 because Bundy clearly stated that his psychopathic behavior was not the result of a dysfunctional home or parents. There was no outward correlation between his mother's rearing and his killing, allegedly, over 100 females. He said that his happenstance introduction to pornography at age 13 lead to an obsession with "The most damaging kind of pornography . . . [which] involves violence and sexual violence."[xviii]

Parents would do well to remember that after we have done our best, our children still have a God-given right to exercise their freedom of choice. Sometimes, their choices bring us much pain and sorrow—just ask God about His highest created being, Lucifer.

HAGGITH (David's Wife #5)

DAY 81

BIBLE TEXT: 2 Samuel 3:4 [David's sons born in Hebron] *And the fourth, Adonijah the son of Haggith . . .*

BIBLE REFERENCES: 2 Samuel 3; 1 Kings 1, 2; 1 Chronicles 3

---

*H*aggith is known for her son, Adonijah, who was David's fourth son. Adonijah determined that he would be David's successor, after Absalom's death. David's first-born son, Amnon, was murdered by David's third-born son, Absalom.

It appears that Amnon, Absalom, and Adonijah inherited only their father's good looks; they did not emulate either David's character or spiritual disposition. The Bible intimates that David, like Eli, the priest, in Hannah's story, did not actively seek to turn his sons' hearts toward submission and obedience to God's will; thus, Eli and David's sons had undisciplined minds and unconverted hearts. Their selfish use and abuse of others to accomplish their self-centered goals were pronounced and decisive.

1 Kings 1 records how Adonijah *exalted himself, saying, I will be king: and he prepared him chariots and horsemen, and fifty men to run before him.* Some of David's long time right-arm men joined Adonijah in openly defying God's expressed will that

Solomon would succeed David. The great feast of Adonijah's self-proclaimed announcement of ascension alerted Nathan, the prophet, to ensure that King David did not delay in taking swift actions to crown Solomon king. Adonijah's end comes during the early years of Solomon's reign (1 Kings 2).

On one hand, parents may not be responsible for encouraging serious character flaws in their children, but on the other hand, some character flaws are both caught and taught. David's experiences role modeled deceit, deception, and lying. While David was quick to repent, Adonijah's decisions demonstrate that he only copied David's rebellious ways.

This is a primary issue regarding children who are exposed to repeated episodes of violence in the home. While mothers may take what they believe are extraordinary steps to shield their children from violent behaviors, studies show that "men who witness their parents' domestic violence are twice as likely to abuse their own wives than sons of nonviolent parents and 50 percent of men who frequently assaulted their wives also frequently abuse their children."[xix]

Likewise, "in families where the mother is assaulted by the father, daughters are at risk of sexual abuse 6.51 times greater than girls in non-abusive families. A child's exposure to the father abusing the mother is the strongest risk factor for transmitting violent behavior from one generation to the next."[xx]

I share this message whenever I conduct workshops on domestic violence because many mothers do not realize that their decisions to stay in abusive relationships for the children's sake ensures that the cycle will continue into the next generation. Children can recover from one episode, but repeated exposure plants seeds which grow into unhealthy behaviors.

BATHSHEBA (David's Wife #8)

DAY 82

BIBLE TEXT: 2 Samuel 11:3 *And David sent and enquired after the woman. And one said, Is not this Bathsheba, the daughter of Eliam, the wife of Uriah the Hittite?*

BIBLE REFERENCES: 2 Samuel 11, 12; 1 Kings 1, 2; 1 Chronicles 1; Matthew 1

---

*B*athsheba, the mother of Solomon, is the last of David's eight wives.[xxi] Michal's father gave her to David, and God punished her for her contempt toward God manifested by her despising David's joyful worship. Abigail sought David, and her wise counsel saved him from *avenging* [himself] *with* [his] *own hand* (1 Samuel 25:33). She was also blessed that her son did not seek to inherit David's throne. How Ahinoam, Maacah, and Haggith came to be David's wives we are not told, but their sons were part of the fourfold curse because David stole Bathsheba from Uriah. Yet, in God's own merciful and gracious manner, Bathsheba was favored by God because He gave David's throne to her son, Solomon.

2 Samuel 11 introduces Bathsheba. She entered David's life the night he stood on his roof top and observed a beautiful woman bathing. Although he learned that she was married, he sent for her

211

and she conceived a son as a result of their one night stand. David tried to pass the child off as Bathsheba's husband's child but her husband, Uriah, a committed solider, refused to sleep with his wife while on leave from battle. David had Uriah carry his own death warrant which instructed that he be placed on the front line of battle.

After Bathsheba mourned for her husband, David "fetched her to his house" and she became his wife. Their child was born and the Bible says, *the thing that David had done displeased the Lord*. While she suffered the loss of her first-born son, there is no indictment against Bathsheba for her part in David's sin. Interestingly, the Bible names only Bathsheba as having four of David's twenty sons (1 Chronicles 3:1-9).

Bathsheba's story is both a reminder of the proportionate allocation of the consequences for sin seen in Eve's story (Genesis 3: 1-6), and a foreshadowing of the proportionate participation in the commission of sin seen in the story of the woman taken in adultery (John 8:1-11). God's judgment is not "one size fits all."

When I sit on the criminal bench, many cases involve co-defendants. Each defendant is usually quick to let me know that others were involved. Why? Because the defendants standing before me want to make sure that their punishments are the same as the others or to complain if they perceive that their sentences are harsher or "unfair." They have a point. The prosecuting attorney should be able to explain, both to the court and to each defendant, why there are any differences in the punishments.

The most dispositive factor is criminal history. Normally, an experienced law breaker is not afforded the same considerations as a first-timer. Experienced criminals use this faulty cost benefit analysis to entice novices to join in unlawful behavior. They argue to the novices that if they are caught, their penalty will not be so bad. The flaw in the analysis is the nature of the crime. Shoplifting is one thing, burglary another, but using a gun in the commission of any crime is in a class all by itself.

DAY 83

BIBLE TEXT: 2 Samuel 12:10 *Now therefore the sword shall never depart from thine house; because thou hast despised me, and hast taken the wife of Uriah the Hittite to be thy wife.*

BIBLE REFERENCES: 2 Samuel 11, 12; 1 Kings 1, 2; 1 Chronicles 1; Matthew 1

---

*B*athsheba suffered in silence for the wrongs David committed against her. David raped her, impregnated her, killed her husband, married her, and caused their son to die. David also suffered in silence because of the wife he had stolen, her innocent husband he had caused to be killed, and the baby he did not really intend to father.

In 2 Samuel 12, the secrets were finally out. Nathan, the prophet, delicately confronted David, using the story of a rich man killing a poor man's only lamb. The Bible records that *David's anger was greatly kindled against the man; and he said to Nathan, As the Lord liveth, the man that hath done this thing shall surely die: And he shall restore the lamb fourfold, because he did this thing, and because he had no pity.*

Thus, David pronounced his own sentence and his private sins were punished "before the sun." God allowed evil to arise in David's own house; the *sword would never depart from* [his] *house*. Through the death of four of his sons, treachery within his own family, and the abuse of his concubines, David suffered the consequences of his sinful decisions.

The first son to die was Bathsheba's son. Later, David's first-born son, Amnon, would be murdered by David's third son, Absalom. Then Absalom would die. Finally, David's fourth son, Adonijah, died as he sought to usurp Solomon's authority as heir to David's throne.

There are two distinct lessons to learn from this episode in David's life: first, our sins will find us out since all things are naked and open to God (Galatians 6:7; Hebrews 4:13); and, second, our sins affect us, our relationship with God, and our ability to deal with sins in others (Psalm 51). Adam and Eve's encounter with God in the cool of the evening confirms that it is best to deal with secrets by just "dealing with them."

We each have a secret or two which are deeply hidden and sometimes even unbeknownst to us. However, the effects of the secrets ooze into our relationships and interactions with others. Secrets exert power over us as we make decisions designed to keep our secrets hidden, such as sexual and physical abuse. Some people, by training, natural instinct, or familiarity with the same secrets, have "x-ray eyes" to clearly see that which we struggle to hide.

Our sins and secrets affect our relationships and communication styles with our children, family, friends, and associates. With our children, we may be too harsh or too lenient with their misconduct as we remember that we acted just like them. We may refrain from pointing out friends' indiscretions because "we've been there and done that!" Or on the other hand, we may be intolerant of others who share our own character traits.

Once (probably lots of times), I was not very understanding of a certain lawyer's presentation. In retrospect, I decided I was not as judicial as I should have been. Now, with every encounter with the lawyer, I must check myself and not act on the desire to bend over backwards to accommodate or appease.

DAY 84

BIBLE TEXT: 2 Samuel 12:24 *And David comforted Bathsheba his wife and went in unto her, and lay with her: and she bare a son, and he called his name Solomon: and the Lord loved him.*

BIBLE REFERENCES: 2 Samuel 11, 12; 1 Kings 1, 2; 1 Chronicles 1; Matthew 1

---

*G*od's love is simply amazing! How completely He forgives and accepts us—one more time! How merciful His promises of hope and encouragement as we pay the penalties for our transgressions and sins. When the prophet Nathan pronounced God's sentence upon David for his great wickedness, their son became very ill. David agonized with God, pleading for the life of their year-old son, but after seven days the child died. Accepting God's will and punishment, David arose and proceeded to get on with his responsibilities.

Then, the Bible says God honored Bathsheba and David with the birth of Solomon. Later, the prophet Nathan told them that God called Solomon Jedidiah, "beloved of Jehovah." God ordained that through this child, this son of David, the Messiah would come. From the very sordid affair, which was the cause of David's great sin, God gave Bathsheba and David hope, and for all humankind a demonstration of God's mercy.

Solomon's reign would be what David's could not be. In grateful joy and appreciation, David wrote Psalm 32:

Psalm 32

1 Count yourself lucky, how happy you must be you get a fresh start, your slate's wiped clean. 2 Count yourself lucky God holds nothing against you and you're holding nothing back from him. 3 When I kept it all inside, my bones turned to powder, my words became daylong groans. 4 The pressure never let up; all the juices of my life dried up. 5 Then I let it all out; I said, "I'll make a clean breast of my failures to God." Suddenly the pressure was gone - my guilt dissolved, my sin disappeared. 6 These things add up. Every one of us needs to pray; when all hell breaks loose and the dam bursts we'll be on high ground, untouched. 7 God's my island hideaway, keeps danger far from the shore, throws garlands of hosannas around my neck. 8 Let me give you some good advice; I'm looking you in the eye and giving it to you straight: 9 "Don't be ornery like a horse or mule that needs bit and bridle to stay on track." 10 God-defiers are always in trouble; God-affirmers find themselves loved every time they turn around. 11 Celebrate God. Sing together everyone! All you honest hearts, raise the roof!

[1]Blessed is he whose transgression is forgiven, whose sin is covered.
[2]Blessed is the man unto whom the LORD imputeth not iniquity, and in whose spirit there is no guile.
[3]When I kept silence, my bones waxed old through my roaring all the day long.
[4]For day and night thy hand was heavy upon me: my moisture is turned into the drought of summer. Selah.
[5]I acknowledge my sin unto thee, and mine iniquity have I not hid. I said, I will confess my transgressions unto the LORD; and thou forgavest the iniquity of my sin. Selah.
[6]For this shall every one that is godly pray unto thee in a time when thou mayest be found: surely in the floods of great waters they shall not come nigh unto him.
[7]Thou art my hiding place; thou shalt preserve me from trouble; thou shalt compass me about with songs of deliverance. Selah.
[8]I will instruct thee and teach thee in the way which thou shalt go: I will guide thee with mine eye.
[9]Be ye not as the horse, or as the mule, which have no understanding: whose mouth must be held in with bit and bridle, lest they come near unto thee.
[10]Many sorrows shall be to the wicked: but he that trusteth in the LORD, mercy shall compass him about.
[11]Be glad in the LORD, and rejoice, ye righteous: and shout for joy, all ye that are upright in heart.

King James Version

DAY 85

BIBLETEXT: 1 Kings 1:11 *Wherefore Nathan spake unto Bathsheba the mother of Solomon, saying, Hast thou not heard that Adonijah the son of Haggith doth reign, and David our lord knoweth it not?*

BIBLE REFERENCES: 2 Samuel 11, 12; 1 Kings 1, 2; 1 Chronicles 1; Matthew 1

---

*A*fter Solomon's birth, nothing more is written about Bathsheba until David's oldest surviving son, Adonijah, plots to usurp David's throne. His scheme placed both Bathsheba and Solomon's lives in danger. Again, God sent the prophet Nathan to address the danger. In 1 Kings 1, Nathan said to Bathsheba, *Now therefore come, let me, I pray thee, give thee counsel, that thou mayest save thine own life, and the life of thy son Solomon.* Her response showed a teachable and obedient disposition; she was insightful and wise.

1 Kings 1 records that David was "very old" and infirmed; Abishag, the Shunammite, a "very fair" damsel, was his personal nurse. Following Nathan's instructions, Bathsheba went into David's bedroom and after she bowed to show respect, David asked her what she wanted. She answered, *My lord, thou swarest by the Lord thy God unto thine handmaid, saying, Assuredly Solomon thy son shall reign after me, and he shall sit upon my throne.*

And now, behold, Adonijah reigneth; and now, my lord the king, thou knowest it not . . . O king, the eyes of all Israel are upon thee, that thou shouldest tell them who shall sit on the throne of my lord the king after him. Otherwise it shall come to pass, when my lord the king shall sleep with his fathers, that I and my son Solomon shall be counted offenders. Nathan came in while she was yet speaking to confirm her story.

Abigail and Bathsheba had kindred spirits. Abigail gave good counsel and Bathsheba accepted good counsel. Her teachable spirit may also explain why her three other sons did not seek to usurp the kingship from Solomon.

I began mentoring in classrooms during my son's third grade year. I must admit that my motives for volunteering were mixed. But for more than twenty years I was involved with students, including students in special dropout prevention programs and those attending underachieving schools. I have worked in public and private schools, with entire classes, small groups, and in one-on-one settings. It does not take long to identify which students have teachable spirits and which ones must be taught to have teachable spirits.

For eight years or so, I volunteered in Reggenia Baskin's second grade classroom at Oakridge Elementary School. One year there was a lad who was used to having each of his idiosyncrasies catered to and every need met. It was clear during our first encounter that we were not on the same page. As the year progressed, the teacher noticed that my weekly hour long contacts were having an inter-esting effect. Since I ignored him and his idiosyncrasies when he attempted to insist upon my accommodation of them, it resulted in helping him to realize that people could and would choose not to facilitate his agenda. His failure to participate in the group activities never stopped the rest of the children's enthusiasm. By the end of the school year, we marveled at his growth in adjusting his behavior to be a part of, rather than distinct from, the cooperating students.

DAY 86

BIBLE TEXT: 1 Kings 1:28 *Then king David answered and said, Call me Bathsheba. And she came into the king's presence, and stood before the king.*

BIBLE REFERENCES: 2 Samuel 11, 12; 1 Kings 1, 2; 1 Chronicles 1; Matthew 1

---

*D*avid moved swiftly in response to the information given by Bathsheba and Nathan. In 1 Kings 1, David *sware, and said, As the Lord liveth, that hath redeemed my soul out of all distress, Even as I sware unto thee by the Lord God of Israel, saying, Assuredly Solomon thy son shall reign after me, and he shall sit upon my throne in my stead; even so will I certainly do this day.*

In respect and with gratitude, *Bathsheba bowed with her face to the earth, and did reverence to the king, and said, Let my lord king David live for ever.* Their plan worked; her cooperation with the prophet Nathan resulted in their desired results. Solomon was immediately installed as king.

I wonder what Bathsheba was really thinking as she appropriately bowed before King David, her husband. Were her thoughts more akin to "Great, you did right by our son!" or "It's about time you did something!" Maybe Bathsheba felt that David really loved her. While David was obeying God's directive that Solomon was to be the next king, David could have also been demonstrating his true love for Bathsheba. Western culture tends to base relationships upon love; "Do you love him or her?" That is the question others most often ask someone who is trying to determine whether to enter, stay, or leave an intimate relationship. But too often the real question is, "What's love got to do with it?"[xxii]

"A person convinced against her will, is unconvinced still," is an old saying. When I was an attorney, I remember often saying "Yes Sir" to judges when I was annoyed with their rulings. My words were disingenuous; they were an unintended verbal cue to myself of how little respect I had for both the ruling and the judge as a person! Eventually, I became aware of this unintentional act and now that I am a judge, if an attorney continues to say "Your Honor," I wonder if the attorney, like me, is using respectful words to cover up a disagreeing spirit. The "respect" for the office does not include the person in the office.

It is very important to me when sentencing defendants to inquire about how they perceive their sentences. My experience shows that when defendants think the court has imposed an unnecessarily harsh sentence, compliance has been problematic. With their lips, defendants "accept" the sentence, but their hearts will not allow them to "cheerfully" comply.

While obedience is demanded of our children, maybe we should thoughtfully consider how they perceive our decisions. Maybe backtalk is their way of letting us know they think they have been treated unfairly. While it may take more time to explain why and how we reached our conclusions and to engage them in the process of determining an appropriate response, the end result is their better understanding and acceptance of the outcome. God does this with us; consider David's punishment for numbering the children of Israel in 1 Chronicles 21.

DAY 87

BIBLE TEXT: 1 King 2:13 *And Adonijah the son of Haggith came to Bathsheba the mother of Solomon. And she said, Comest thou peaceably? And he said, Peaceably.*

BIBLE REFERENCES: 2 Samuel 11, 12; 1 Kings 1, 2; 1 Chronicles 1; Matthew 1

---

*A*fter Solomon was crowned king, 1 Kings 2 states that Adonijah approached Bathsheba and asked her to talk to Solomon on his behalf. Bathsheba asked Adonijah if he came peaceably since she knew his character and history and was cautious about any interactions with him.

Adonijah begins by telling Bathsheba that *Thou knowest that the kingdom was mine, and that all Israel set their faces on me, that I should reign: howbeit the kingdom is turned about, and is become my brother's: for it was his from the Lord.* He wanted as his wife David's personal nurse, Abishag, the Shunammite. He was confident that Solomon would not deny his mother's request on Adonijah's behalf.

This really is an interesting incident in Bathsheba's life. Was her response based upon her being sly like a fox or dumb like a sheep? Did she understand the implications of Adonijah's request, letting him think that he was using her, when she knew full well the consequences of his request? Or was she again a hapless victim, a pawn in a powerful man's indiscretion?

As queen mother, she also knew court protocol. I think she was wise and insightful, allowing events set in motion by others to run their courses. Her response to Adonijah's request supports that she was as crafty as Adonijah.

When I was a freshman in college, I was madly in love with a handsome, smart, intelligent boyfriend who had a bright and successful future. Surely, he was my husband to be! But then I chose to study abroad my sophomore year, hoping that the relationship would survive our school-year-long separation. It did survive during our separation, but the relationship ended when he visited me after I returned home. After he arrived back at the college, he called and asked me to consider our getting back together.

With a broken heart, I sought my father's advice. He said to tell him, "The relationship is exactly where you left it." As a 21 year-old, whether that was the best advice or not, I did not know. But I trusted my father and followed his recommendation. My father's assessment was burned into my psyche and his advice has added texture to the fabric of my life.

We all have made and are making choices which have serious and significant consequences. Those consequences almost always cannot be side-stepped or undone even when we are remorseful and truly sorry. When someone loves and cares about us, they warn us of the possible negative outcomes and dangers of our proposed plans, encouraging us to rethink our solutions.

DAY 88

BIBLE TEXT: 1 Kings 2:19 *Bathsheba therefore went unto king Solomon, to speak unto him for Adonijah. And the king rose up to meet her, and bowed himself unto her, and sat down on his throne, and caused a seat to be set for the king's mother; and she sat on his right hand.*

BIBLE REFERENCES: 2 Samuel 11, 12; 1 Kings 1, 2; 1 Chronicles 1; Matthew 1

What great reverence, respect, and honor Solomon showed toward his mother as she came before him with Adonijah's request. Solomon bowed to her! Then he ordered a seat for her to sit on his right hand.

Solomon knew his parents' story and that he was born after David pronounced his own fourfold punishment (2 Samuel 11 and 12). Solomon also knew that the prophet Nathan had announced that God loved him and ordained that he would succeed his father. Solomon knew that Bathsheba had interceded on his behalf to ensure that he was crowned king. It was easy for him to show loving respect to his mother.

Bathsheba prefaced her request so that Solomon had committed himself to grant it, even before he knew what it was. As she spoke to her son, was she naively just conveying the message? Was she hesitant about Solomon's response to Adonijah's request? Or was she confident that Solomon would appropriately handle the situation, allowing her to keep her word to Adonijah, while putting an end to his ability to undermine Solomon's reign? What was she thinking as she said, *Let Abishag the Shunammite be given to Adonijah thy brother to wife.* There was silence as her words penetrated the air and Solomon's ears. His mind captured both her spoken and unspoken words.

When my siblings and I were growing up, we sometimes needed to avoid a friend's invitation to go someplace or do something we did not want to do. In those situations, we would walk up to mother and say, "Mother, say no." She always obliged. Then "sorrowfully" we could and would tell our friends that mother said "No." She provided the authoritative end to the discussion. (That was back in the day when children did not challenge parents' authority!)

Yet, even today, it would be a good thing if children, when asked why they choose not to make a poor decision, could say confidently and authoritatively, "My parents won't let me!" It would not be a statement of fear, but rather one of assurance as children learned that they could count on their parents to back them up and support them against "the world."

Often while conducting domestic violence court, it was clear to me that for one party the relationship was over and the other side "didn't get it." From the bench, I allowed the leaving party to turn to the other and clearly state that the relationship was over. Then, I explained to the holding-on party that he/she had to accept at face value these facts and move on. Any further attempts to have contact with the leaving party would most likely result in incarceration. For most respondents, the thought of jail versus having contact resulted in clearer thinking and appropriate choices.

Often after such hearings, I thought to myself, I just played the role of my mother saying, "No."

DAY 89

BIBLE TEXT: 1 Kings 2:22 *And king Solomon answered and said unto his mother, And why dost thou ask Abishag the Shunammite for Adonijah? ask for him the kingdom also; for he is mine elder brother; even for him, and for Abiathar the priest, and for Joab the son of Zeruiah.*

BIBLE REFERENCES: 2 Samuel 11, 12; 1 Kings 1, 2; 1 Chronicles 1; Matthew 1

Was Bathsheba surprised or pleased with Solomon's response to her request? Solomon asked her why she made the request on Adonijah's behalf. Adonijah knew that his request for David's last wife or concubine was tantamount to asking for the kingdom. A clear sign of a new king's power and reign was to assume the wives and concubines of the previous king, as David did when he succeeded King Saul (2 Samuel 12:8).

During Absalom's revolt, he openly violated the ten concubines David left behind when he fled Jerusalem (2 Samuel 16:20-22). Bathsheba knew that David afterwards banished the concubines into a life of widowhood (2 Samuel 20:3).

Was Solomon really stunned by Bathsheba's request or was he feigning surprise? Was his retort more like Jesus' response to the Syrophenician woman recorded in Mark 7:25-30? A definitive answer to that question would shed light on Bathsheba's motives.

Was Bathsheba tricked by Adonijah or tricking Adonijah? Either way, Solomon appreciated the significance of Adonijah's request, concluding that Adonijah had *spoken this word against his own life . . . Adonijah shall be put to death this day.* Again, Bathsheba (whether sly as a fox or dumb as a sheep) had protected and ensured the kingdom for her son.

Oswald Chambers wrote in *Studies in the Sermon on the Mount* that "God never threatens; the devil never warns." While we may sometimes use the words interchangeably, they are not synonymous. Bathsheba warned Solomon of Adonijah's threat to Solomon's reign as David's successor. Threats are issued to get people to do what we want them to do. Warnings are given to get people to do what they should do.

As I advise defendants about the terms of probation imposed as a part of their sentences, I use a mixture of warnings and threats. For example, instead of being ordered to jail, defendants may complete jail work-camp days, which require them to wear striped uniforms and pick up trash along the roadsides. But defendants must schedule their work-camp days. Those who procrastinate run the risk of not having the days completed and most likely will be sentenced to jail days in excess of the number of jail work-camp days. That part is a threat (albeit a real threat) to get them to do what I want them to do, i.e., complete the jail work-camp days. But the warning to sign up early and get their conditions completed in a timely manner is encouragement to do what is in their best interest.

We would do well to listen to ourselves as we talk to our children, in particular, and others, in general, to isolate threats from warnings. Too often we issue threats because we want someone else's behavior to benefit us. Consider the response, "Do as I say, because I said to!"

Warnings, on the other hand, are given with love and concern. We want others to do their best because it protects them from danger, harm, and inevitable consequences.

DAY 90

BIBLE TEXT: Matthew 1:6 *And Jesse begat David the king; and David the king begat Solomon of her that had been the wife of Urias.*

BIBLE REFERENCES: 2 Samuel 11, 12; 1 Kings 1, 2; 1 Chronicles 1; Matthew 1

O *f her that had been the wife of Urias.* Matthew identified by name Tamar, Rahab, and Ruth; why was Bathsheba identified only by her first husband? What made her adultery so different from Tamar, who allowed Judah, her father-in-law, to treat her as if she were a prostitute (Genesis 38:6-30)? Or from Rahab, who was a harlot (Joshua 2)?

David sinned against Bathsheba, so maybe Bathsheba was not named because even centuries later King David's sin was too painful; there was no need to bring any more attention than necessary to their story. But, God ordained that Bathsheba was one of the five women included in the genealogy of Christ.

Count on it—when others seek to marginalize us because of our sordid past, God confirms and reaffirms how He feels about us. What others think about us is not dispositive with God. Their opinions about our past sins and transgressions, which they choose to hold against us, hold them back from moving into their glorious future.

As we confess our sins, God reveals the future He desires for us. Because of our forgiven and forgotten past, our grateful hearts compel us to offer only praise, worship, thankfulness, and adoration. Our lips and hearts ponder God's amazing grace, matchless love and undeserved favor! Whenever we find ourselves offering little praise, worship, thankfulness, and adoration, we should pause and reflect upon God's amazing grace, matchless love and undeserved favor.

There is much wisdom in learning from the mistakes and choices of others. It is unwise to personally test every theory about the best way to live. Yet, many people believe that only those who have experienced the temptation are best qualified to help those in similar conditions. If this were so, God would not have specifically instructed Adam and Eve to "not eat" of "the tree of knowledge of good and evil" (Genesis 2:16, 17). Nor, would it have been necessary for Jesus to include in the Lord's Prayer that we ask not to be led "into temptation, but deliver us from evil" (Matthew 6:13).

The entire plan of salvation was instituted to save us from the predicament we are in because Adam did not (and we do not) obey God's clear instructions. That is what is so amazing about grace! God found a way to save us in spite of ourselves and He treats us as if we had always obeyed! Just imagine what it would be like if we always chose to obey; read about the blessings of Deuteronomy 28.

God's grace extends to each of us, whether our name is or is not recorded for others to see.

What incredible new insights from these women's amazing old stories!

INDEX

END NOTES

i.   (Day 26) Pauline, Jon. *The Gospel From Patmos*. Review and Herald Publishing Association, 2007.

ii. (Day 27) R. T. Kendall, *Total Forgiveness,* Charisma House, 2002.

iii. (Day 40) *The Clear Word*. Review and Herald, 1994.

iv. (Day 43) http:// burn24-7.com/2011/ the-song-writes-you-story-on-more-than-enough/

v.   (Day 55) *New Life Bible*. Christian Literature International, 1969.

vi. (Day 55) *Contemporary English Version Bible*. American Bible Society. 1995.

vii. (Day 55) *New International Reader*. Biblica, 1996, 1998.

viii. (Day 55) *The Clear Word*. Review and Herald, 1994.

ix. (Day 55) *The Message*. NavPress Publishing Group, 2002.

x.   (Day 55) http://dictionary.cambridge.org/

xi. (Day 59) Ellen White. *Desire of Ages*, pps. 347-348. Pacific Press Publishing Association.

xii. (Day 60) LeRoy Froom, *Coming of the Comforter*, p. 94. Review and Herald Publishing Association, 1956.

xiii. (Day 64) www.achristianhome.com/Good_Things/

FunnyFunny/ a_white_lie_church_cake.htm

xiv. (Day 74) www.natefacs.org/JFCSE/v17no1/v17no1Morris. pdf *Transition to Marriage: A Literature Review marriage partners selecting mates with similar personality*

xv. (Day 76) *But if a woman have long hair, it is a glory to her: for her hair is given her for a covering* (1 Corinthians 11:15).

xvi. (Day 79) www.cnn.com/2007/HEALTH/family/10/12/par. birth.order/index.html

xvii. (Day 80) http://en.wikipedia.org/wiki/Geshur

xviii. (Day 80) http://www.pureintimacy.org/gr/intimacy/understanding/a0000082.cfm

xix. (Day 81) Http://devbehavpeds.ouhsc.edu/assets/pdf/CPT/ The%20Effects%20of%20Domestic20Violence%20on%20 Children-ppt.pdf

xx. (Day 81) http://www.acadv.org/children.html

xxi. (Day 82) 1 Samuel 19:11; 2 Samuel 3:2-5; 11:17.

xxii. (Day 86) The question is taken from a 1993 movie by that name about the relationship of Ike and Tina Turner.